DEALING WITH MANIPULATIVE PEOPLE IN RELATIONSHIPS

A Guide to Understand and Overcome Manipulation

VICTORY KATE NANCY

INTRODUCTION

The Nature of Manipulation

Manipulation in relationships is a tricky concept, often hidden in plain sight. It occurs when one person uses unfair methods to control or influence another person's thoughts, feelings, or behaviors. This can happen in many ways, some obvious, some not so much, but all forms of manipulation share the common goal of gaining power over someone else. Understanding manipulation is key to recognizing it in your own relationships and taking steps to protect yourself.

At its core, manipulation is about control. The manipulator, whether consciously or unconsciously, tries to shape the other person's behavior to suit their own needs. This control can be exercised in many ways, ranging from subtle suggestions to outright demands. The problem is that manipulation often involves deceit, emotional pressure, or other forms of unfair influence, making it hard for the person being manipulated to see what's happening.

One of the most common forms of manipulation is emotional manipulation. This occurs when someone uses your emotions against you to get what they want. For instance, they might guilt you into doing something by saying things like, "If you really loved me, you would do this," or they might play the victim, making you feel sorry for them even when they're in the wrong. Emotional manipulators often make you feel responsible for their happiness or wellbeing, which can lead you to make decisions that are more about keeping them satisfied than about what's best for you.

Another form of manipulation is psychological manipulation, where someone distorts your perception of reality to maintain control. This can include tactics like gaslighting, where the manipulator denies reality or twists the truth to make you doubt your memory, judgment, or sanity.

For example, if you confront them about something hurtful they did, they might completely deny it or claim that you're "imagining things." Over time, this can erode your confidence in your own thoughts and feelings, making you more dependent on the manipulator for a sense of reality.

Behavioral manipulation is another way people exert control in relationships. This involves the manipulator using actions, or threats of actions, to influence your behavior. For instance, they might withhold affection, give you the silent treatment, or make you feel guilty as a way to get you to comply with their wishes. Behavioral manipulation can be subtle, like a disappointed sigh when you don't do what they want, or overt, like threatening to leave you if you don't comply. The goal is to make you feel uneasy or insecure, so you're more likely to give in to their demands.

Manipulation can also take the form of social manipulation, where the manipulator tries to control who you interact with or how others perceive you. This can include isolating you from friends and family, spreading rumors, or turning people against you. By controlling your social environment, the manipulator makes you more dependent on them and less likely to seek support from others. Social manipulation can be particularly harmful because it not only affects your relationship with the manipulator but also your relationships with others.

Sometimes, manipulation is very subtle, almost imperceptible, especially when it involves covert manipulation. Covert manipulators are often very skilled at hiding their true intentions. They might use flattery, feigned concern, or seemingly innocent questions to steer you in a particular direction. For instance, they might say, "I'm just looking out for you," while subtly discouraging you from pursuing a goal that doesn't align with their interests. Covert manipulation can be hard to detect because it often comes across as caring or supportive, but the underlying intent is to control or influence you.

In contrast, overt manipulation is more direct and easier to recognize. This might involve obvious threats, demands, or ultimatums, where the manipulator makes it clear what they want and the consequences of not complying. Overt manipulators might use intimidation or bullying tactics, such as raising their voice, making threats, or using physical force to get their way. While overt manipulation is more apparent, it can still be very effective, especially if the person being manipulated feels vulnerable or powerless.

Manipulators often rely on a combination of these tactics to maintain control. For instance, they might use emotional manipulation to make you feel guilty, then follow it up with behavioral manipulation by giving you the silent treatment until you give in. Or they might use social manipulation to isolate you, making it easier to use psychological manipulation without interference from others. The overlapping nature of these tactics can make it difficult to recognize the manipulation as it's happening.

Understanding manipulation also means recognizing the impact it has on relationships. Manipulation creates an imbalance of power, where the manipulator holds most of the control and the other person is left feeling confused, anxious, or insecure. This imbalance can lead to a host of negative outcomes, including diminished self-esteem, increased stress, and even physical or emotional harm. Over time, the person being manipulated may begin to doubt their own worth, making it even harder to stand up to the manipulator or seek help.

Manipulation can also be self-perpetuating. The more the manipulator gets away with their behavior, the more likely they are to continue using it. Meanwhile, the person being manipulated may become more entrenched in the cycle, feeling increasingly trapped and helpless. This cycle can be difficult to break, especially if the manipulation has been going on for a long time or if the manipulator is someone you care about deeply.

However, it's important to understand that manipulation is a learned behavior. People aren't born manipulative; they learn these tactics over time, often as a way to cope with their own insecurities or to achieve their goals. This doesn't excuse manipulative behavior, but it does offer insight into why some people might resort to these tactics. Understanding this can be helpful when it comes to addressing manipulation in your own relationships.

One of the key steps in dealing with manipulation is awareness. The more you understand about manipulation and how it works, the better equipped you'll be to recognize it in your relationships. This awareness can empower you to take action, whether that means setting boundaries, seeking support, or even ending the relationship if necessary. It's also important to remember that you have the right to be treated with respect and to have your thoughts, feelings, and boundaries honored in a relationship.

While manipulation can be damaging, it's also something that can be overcome. By educating yourself, building your self-esteem, and learning to recognize manipulative behaviors, you can protect yourself from manipulation and build healthier, more balanced relationships. It's not always easy, but taking these steps can lead to a greater sense of empowerment and peace in your relationships.

Manipulation in relationships is about control and can manifest in many forms, from emotional and psychological tactics to behavioral and social pressures. Whether overt or covert, manipulation creates an imbalance of power that can harm the person being manipulated. By understanding the nature of manipulation and its impact on relationships, you can take steps to protect yourself and foster healthier interactions with others.

The Impact of Manipulation

Manipulation in relationships can deeply affect a person on many levels, including emotionally, mentally, and physically. These effects often happen gradually, making them harder to notice until they have already caused significant damage. Understanding these impacts is crucial for anyone trying to recognize and break free from manipulative behavior.

Emotionally, manipulation can lead to a rollercoaster of feelings, often leaving the person being manipulated feeling drained, confused, and uncertain about their emotions. One common emotional effect is constant guilt. Manipulators often use tactics like guilt-tripping, where they make you feel responsible for their happiness or well-being. For example, if you don't do what they want, they might say things like, "You don't care about me," or "I thought you loved me." Over time, this guilt can weigh heavily on you, making you feel like you're always doing something wrong, even when you're not.

Another emotional impact is anxiety. When you're in a relationship with a manipulator, you might start to feel anxious because you never know what to expect. The manipulator might change their behavior suddenly, going from kind and loving to cold and distant without any clear reason. This unpredictability can make you feel constantly on edge, worrying about how to keep the peace or avoid upsetting them. This anxiety can spill over into other areas of your life, affecting your ability to focus, sleep, or even enjoy things that used to make you happy.

Mentally, manipulation can be even more damaging because it often targets your thoughts and beliefs about yourself. One of the most harmful effects is self-doubt. Manipulators are skilled at making you question your own judgment and perceptions. For instance, if you confront them about something they did, they might deny it completely or twist the facts, making you wonder if you imagined it or misunderstood what happened. This tactic, known as gaslighting, can make you feel like you can't trust your own mind. Over time, this constant self-doubt can erode your confidence, leaving you feeling powerless and dependent on the manipulator for validation.

Another mental effect is confusion. Manipulators often send mixed messages or contradict themselves, making it hard to understand what they really want or mean. They might say one thing but do another, or change their demands based on what suits them at the moment. This can create a confusing environment where you're constantly second-guessing your actions and decisions, trying to figure out how to please them or avoid conflict. This confusion can be mentally exhausting, leaving you feeling overwhelmed and unsure of where you stand in the relationship.

Physically, the stress and emotional turmoil caused by manipulation can manifest in various ways. Chronic stress is a common physical effect, and it can lead to a range of health problems. When you're constantly stressed, your body is in a state of heightened alert, which can lead to headaches, stomach issues, and even weakened immune function. Over time, this stress can also contribute to more serious conditions like high blood pressure, heart disease, or chronic pain. The connection between stress and physical health is well-documented, and the ongoing strain of dealing with manipulation can take a significant toll on your body.

Sleep problems are another physical effect of manipulation. When you're worried or anxious about your relationship, it can be hard to relax and get a good night's sleep. You might find yourself lying awake at night, replaying conversations in your head, or worrying about what will happen next. Lack of sleep can make everything feel worse, affecting your mood, energy levels, and ability to think clearly. This can create a vicious cycle where poor sleep makes it harder to cope with the stress of the relationship, and the stress makes it harder to sleep.

The emotional, mental, and physical impacts of manipulation are interconnected, creating a cycle that can be hard to break. For example, the emotional stress of feeling guilty or anxious can lead to mental exhaustion and self-doubt, which in turn can cause physical symptoms like headaches or fatigue. As these effects build up, they can start to affect other areas of your life, such as your work, friendships, and overall sense of well-being.

One real-life example of these impacts can be seen in the story of a woman named Sarah, who was in a relationship with a manipulative partner. Over time, Sarah began to notice that she was always feeling guilty, even about things that weren't her fault. Her partner would often make comments like, "You're so selfish," or "You never think about anyone but yourself," whenever she tried to set boundaries or take care of her own needs. This constant guilt made Sarah feel like she was a bad person, and she started to doubt her own judgment.

Sarah also began to experience physical symptoms, like constant headaches and trouble sleeping. She was always on edge, worrying about what her partner would say or do next. The stress of the relationship began to affect her job, as she found it harder to focus and complete tasks. She also started to pull away from friends and family, feeling too exhausted and embarrassed to explain what was going on.

Psychologically, manipulation often leads to learned helplessness, a condition where the person being manipulated starts to believe that they have no control over their situation. This is a common outcome of long-term manipulation, especially when the manipulator uses tactics like gaslighting or isolation. When someone is manipulated into thinking that their feelings, thoughts, or actions don't matter or won't make a difference, they may stop trying to change their situation altogether. This can make it even harder to break free from the manipulative relationship, as the person may feel trapped and hopeless.

The power dynamics in a manipulative relationship also play a significant role in the effects on the individual. The manipulator holds most of the power, while the person being manipulated is often left feeling powerless and dependent. This power imbalance can lead to feelings of low self-esteem and worthlessness. When someone is constantly told or shown that their feelings don't matter, or that they're not good enough, they may start to believe it. This can lead to a cycle of negative self-talk and a diminished sense of self-worth.

In addition to the individual effects, manipulation can also have a ripple effect on other relationships and areas of life. For example, someone who has been manipulated in a romantic relationship may find it difficult to trust others, even after the manipulative relationship has ended. They may carry the emotional and psychological scars into new relationships, making it hard to form healthy, trusting connections. This can lead to a sense of isolation and loneliness, further exacerbating the emotional and mental effects of the manipulation.

The impact of manipulation in relationships is profound and far-reaching. Emotionally, it can lead to feelings of guilt, anxiety, and confusion. Mentally, it can cause self-doubt, loss of confidence, and learned helplessness. Physically, the stress of being manipulated can manifest in health problems like chronic stress, sleep issues, and even more serious conditions. Understanding these impacts is the first step in recognizing manipulation and taking steps to protect yourself. By acknowledging the emotional, mental, and physical toll that manipulation takes, you can begin to rebuild your sense of self-worth and move towards healthier, more balanced relationships.

CHAPTER 1

Recognizing Manipulative Behavior

Types of Manipulators

In relationships, manipulators can take on various forms, each with distinct characteristics and behaviors. Understanding the different types of manipulators is essential to recognizing when you might be dealing with one. Some of the most common types of manipulators include covert, overt, and passive-aggressive manipulators. Each type operates differently, but all share the goal of controlling or influencing others to serve their own needs.

Covert manipulators are often the most difficult to identify because their tactics are subtle and often disguised as care or concern. They tend to work behind the scenes, influencing your thoughts and actions in ways that are not immediately obvious. Covert manipulators are often charming and personable, making it hard to believe they might be manipulating you. They might use flattery, kindness, or a seemingly genuine interest in your well-being to gain your trust. However, their true intent is to control you, often without you realizing it.

A hallmark of covert manipulation is gaslighting. Gaslighting is when someone makes you doubt your own perception of reality. For example, if you express concern about something they did, they might deny it ever happened or suggest that you're being overly sensitive. Over time, this can make you question your memory, judgment, and even your sanity. Covert manipulators might also use guilt-tripping, making you feel responsible for their emotions or actions. They might say things like, "I just want what's best for you," while subtly steering you in the direction that benefits them. The covert manipulator's strength lies in their ability to hide their true intentions, making their behavior difficult to detect.

Overt manipulators, on the other hand, are much more direct in their approach. Their tactics are obvious and often involve a clear display of power or control. Overt manipulators might use intimidation, threats, or outright demands to get what they want. They are often less concerned with how they are perceived by others, focusing instead on achieving their goals as quickly as possible. Overt manipulation can include behaviors such as bullying, where the manipulator uses aggressive tactics to force you into submission. This might involve raising their voice, using demeaning language, or physically intimidating you to make you comply with their wishes.

Another common tactic of overt manipulators is emotional blackmail. Emotional blackmail involves using threats or ultimatums to control your behavior. For example, they might say, "If you don't do this, I'll leave you," or "If you really loved me, you would do what I ask." These statements are designed to pressure you into doing something you're uncomfortable with, by making you fear the consequences of saying no. Overt manipulators are often very clear about their demands, leaving little room for negotiation or discussion. Their goal is to dominate the relationship, ensuring that their needs are always met, often at the expense of your own.

Passive-aggressive manipulators fall somewhere between covert and overt manipulators, using indirect methods to express their discontent or to control a situation. Passive-aggressive behavior involves expressing negative feelings in a subtle, indirect way rather than addressing them openly. This can include behaviors like giving the silent treatment, making sarcastic comments, or deliberately doing something poorly to avoid responsibility. Passive-aggressive manipulators often use these tactics as a way to express anger or frustration without having to confront the issue directly.

One common passive-aggressive tactic is silent treatment. This occurs when the manipulator refuses to communicate with you as a way to punish you or get their way. They might stop talking to you for hours, days, or even longer, leaving you feeling confused and anxious about what you did wrong. The silent treatment can be incredibly stressful because it leaves you in a state of uncertainty, wondering what you did to upset them and how you can fix it. The goal is to make you feel guilty or desperate enough to apologize or give in to their demands, even if you're not sure what those demands are.

Another passive-aggressive behavior is sarcasm or backhanded compliments. These are comments that seem like praise on the surface but have a hidden negative message. For example, a passive-aggressive manipulator might say, "It's nice to see you finally made an effort," implying that you usually don't. These comments can leave you feeling hurt or confused, especially if you're not sure whether the manipulator is being sincere or not. Passive-aggressive manipulators often use sarcasm as a way to express their dissatisfaction without having to directly address the issue, making it difficult for you to respond or defend yourself.

Each type of manipulator uses different tactics, but the goal is always the same: to control or influence you to meet their needs. Recognizing these behaviors is the first step in protecting yourself from manipulation. It's important to understand that manipulation is not always intentional. Some people might use these tactics because they've learned them from others or because they don't know how to communicate their needs in a healthier way. However, this does not excuse manipulative behavior, and it's crucial to set boundaries and protect yourself if you notice these patterns in your relationships.

One example of covert manipulation could be a partner who constantly praises you for being "so understanding" when they make mistakes, subtly implying that you should always forgive them, no matter what. This can create a dynamic where you feel obligated to overlook their behavior, even when it's harmful to you. An example of overt manipulation might be a partner who demands that you quit your job because they want you to stay home, using threats of ending the relationship if you refuse. In a passive-aggressive scenario, a partner might agree to do something you ask but then do it poorly on purpose, so you're less likely to ask them again.

Recognizing the different types of manipulators and their tactics can help you better understand your relationships and take steps to protect yourself. Whether the manipulation is covert, overt, or passive-aggressive, the key is to recognize the signs and address them early on. Setting clear boundaries, communicating openly, and seeking support from trusted friends or professionals can help you navigate these challenges and build healthier, more balanced relationships.

Red Flags and Warning Signs

Recognizing red flags and warning signs in a relationship is essential for identifying manipulative behavior before it causes significant harm. Manipulators often use specific tactics to control or influence their partners, and being aware of these behaviors can help you protect yourself. These red flags can be subtle at first, but over time, they become more evident as the manipulative patterns repeat.

One of the most common red flags is constant criticism. A manipulator may frequently criticize you, often under the guise of being "helpful" or "honest." This criticism can target various aspects of your life, including your appearance, decisions, or personality. For example, they might say things like, "You'd be so much prettier if you just lost a little weight," or "You're too sensitive; you need to toughen up." These comments are meant to undermine your confidence and make you feel inadequate. Over time, constant criticism can erode your self-esteem, making you more dependent on the manipulator for validation.

Another warning sign is isolation from friends and family. Manipulators often try to cut you off from your support network, making it easier for them to control you. They might do this by subtly discouraging you from spending time with loved ones or by creating conflicts that make it difficult for you to maintain those relationships. For example, they might complain that your friends don't like them or that your family is too demanding of your time. Over time, you might find yourself seeing less of the people who care about you, leaving you more reliant on the manipulator for emotional support. This isolation can make it harder for you to recognize the manipulation and seek help.

Blaming and scapegoating are also common tactics used by manipulators. They rarely take responsibility for their actions and are quick to blame others, especially their partner, for any problems that arise. If something goes wrong, they might say things like, "This is all your fault," or "If you hadn't done that, we wouldn't be in this situation." This constant blaming can make you feel guilty and responsible for issues that aren't your fault. Over time, you might start to believe that you are the cause of all the problems in the relationship, further undermining your confidence and making you more susceptible to manipulation.

Emotional blackmail is another red flag to watch out for. Manipulators use emotional blackmail to control your behavior by playing on your fears, guilt, or compassion. They might make threats like, "If you leave me, I'll hurt myself," or "If you don't do this for me, I'll never speak to you again." These threats are designed to make you feel trapped and force you to comply with their demands. Emotional blackmail can be incredibly stressful, as it puts you in a position where you feel you have no choice but to give in to their wishes to avoid negative consequences.

Another common tactic is gaslighting, where the manipulator makes you question your reality. They might deny things they've said or done, make you doubt your memory, or suggest that you're overreacting or imagining things. For example, if you confront them about something hurtful they said, they might respond with, "I never said that, you must be remembering it wrong," or "You're being too emotional; it wasn't that bad." Over time, this can make you doubt your perception of events and even your sanity, making it easier for the manipulator to control you.

Love-bombing is another red flag that can be difficult to recognize because it initially feels positive. Love-bombing involves overwhelming you with affection, attention, and gifts early in the relationship. The manipulator may shower you with compliments, make grand gestures, or say things like, "You're the best thing that ever happened to me," or "I've never felt this way about anyone before." While this can feel flattering, it's often a tactic to quickly establish control and create a sense of obligation. Once the manipulator feels they have you hooked, the love-bombing often stops, and the more manipulative behaviors begin to emerge.

Jealousy and possessiveness are also warning signs of manipulation. While it's natural to feel a little jealous in a relationship, manipulators take this to an extreme. They may become overly possessive, constantly questioning where you are, who you're with, and what you're doing. They might say things like, "I just love you so much, I can't stand the thought of losing you," or "I'm only jealous because

I care about you." However, this behavior is more about control than love. The manipulator uses jealousy to keep you on edge and to limit your interactions with others, making it easier to isolate you and maintain control.

Withholding affection or approval is another tactic manipulators use to keep you in line. They might give you the silent treatment, refuse to show affection, or withdraw their approval when you do something they don't like. For example, if you don't agree with them on something, they might suddenly become cold or distant, making you feel anxious and desperate to get back in their good graces. This behavior conditions you to seek their approval and avoid doing anything that might upset them, even if it means compromising your own needs or values.

Financial control is a more tangible form of manipulation, where the manipulator controls or restricts your access to money. They might insist on managing all the finances, give you an allowance, or criticize your spending habits. In more extreme cases, they might prevent you from working or accessing your own money, making you financially dependent on them. This financial control can make it very difficult to leave the relationship, as you might fear being unable to support yourself without their help.

Inconsistent behavior is another red flag. Manipulators often switch between being loving and supportive to being critical or distant. This inconsistency keeps you off balance, never knowing what to expect. One moment they might be showering you with affection, and the next they might be ignoring you or picking a fight. This unpredictable behavior can be very confusing and stressful, as you're constantly trying to figure out what you did to cause the change and how you can get back to the positive side of their attention.

Testing boundaries is a tactic where the manipulator gradually pushes your limits to see how much they can get away with. They might start with small requests or demands, then slowly increase their expectations. For example, they might first ask you to cancel plans with friends to spend time with them, and later expect you to stop seeing those friends altogether. By testing your boundaries in this way, they slowly erode your sense of autonomy and make it easier to control you.

Recognizing these red flags is crucial for identifying manipulative behavior in a relationship. It's important to trust your instincts and pay attention to how you feel in the relationship. If you notice any of these warning signs, it might be a sign that the relationship is unhealthy, and it's worth taking a step back to evaluate whether it's truly serving your well-being. Seeking support from trusted friends, family, or a therapist can also help you gain perspective and take steps to protect yourself from manipulation. Remember, healthy relationships are based on mutual respect, trust, and open communication, not on control and manipulation.

The Psychology Behind Manipulation

Manipulative behavior is often driven by deep-seated psychological factors that influence how individuals interact with others. Understanding these factors can help us comprehend why some people resort to manipulation in their relationships. While the exact reasons can vary, certain patterns and motivations are commonly observed among manipulators.

One of the primary psychological reasons for manipulation is the desire for control. Manipulators often feel a need to control others to feel secure or powerful. This need for control can stem from various sources, such as childhood experiences where they may have felt powerless or out of control. By manipulating others, they create a sense of dominance, which provides them with the security and confidence they crave. For some, this control compensates for feelings of inadequacy or low self-esteem, allowing them to assert their influence over others as a way to boost their own self-worth.

Manipulators often have a lack of empathy, which plays a significant role in their behavior. Empathy is the ability to understand and share the feelings of others, and it acts as a natural barrier against manipulative actions. However, individuals who lack empathy may struggle to see the impact of their behavior on others. They might view relationships more as transactions or opportunities to get what they want, rather than as connections based on mutual care and respect. Without empathy, they are less likely to feel guilt or remorse for their actions, making it easier for them to manipulate others without concern for the emotional damage they cause.

Another psychological factor that can lead to manipulative behavior is insecurity. Many manipulators are deeply insecure and use manipulation as a way to protect themselves from perceived threats. For example, someone who is insecure about their worth in a relationship might use tactics like guilt-tripping or emotional blackmail to keep their partner from leaving them. By making the other person feel responsible for their emotions, the manipulator can create a sense of dependence, ensuring that their partner stays with them despite their insecurities. This type of manipulation often arises from a fear of abandonment or rejection, where the manipulator believes that controlling their partner is the only way to maintain the relationship.

The need for validation is another driving force behind manipulative behavior. Manipulators often seek constant validation from others to reinforce their sense of self-worth. This can lead them to engage in behaviors like love-bombing, where they shower their partner with affection and praise to receive the same in return. This cycle of seeking validation can become addictive, as the manipulator relies on external approval to feel good about themselves. When they don't receive the validation they crave, they may resort to more manipulative tactics to extract it, such as playing the victim or creating drama to elicit sympathy.

Some manipulators are driven by narcissism, a personality trait characterized by an inflated sense of self-importance and a lack of regard for others. Narcissistic manipulators often believe that they are entitled to special treatment and will go to great lengths to ensure they get it. They may use manipulation to maintain their image, control their environment, or achieve their goals without considering the impact on others. Narcissists often view relationships as a means to an end, using others to fulfill their own needs for attention, admiration, or power. Their manipulation is often more calculated and deliberate, as they see others as tools to be used rather than as equals in a relationship.

In some cases, manipulators may also suffer from personality disorders, such as borderline personality disorder or antisocial personality disorder. These disorders can contribute to manipulative behavior, as they often involve difficulties in forming healthy relationships and regulating emotions. For instance, someone with borderline personality disorder may fear abandonment so intensely that they engage in manipulative behaviors to keep their partner close. On the other hand, someone with antisocial personality disorder may lack a conscience and manipulate others purely for personal gain, without any regard for the consequences.

Learned behavior can also play a significant role in why people become manipulators. If someone grows up in an environment where manipulation was common, they may come to see it as a normal way to interact with others. For example, a child who witnesses a parent using guilt or coercion to get their way may internalize these tactics and use them in their own relationships later in life. This learned behavior can be difficult to unlearn, especially if the individual doesn't recognize it as problematic. They may genuinely believe that manipulation is an acceptable or even necessary way to achieve their goals.

Another factor contributing to manipulative behavior is the manipulator's fear of vulnerability. Some individuals are uncomfortable with being open and honest in their relationships because they fear being hurt, rejected, or exposed. To protect themselves, they may use manipulation as a way to keep others at a distance or to maintain control over how they are perceived. By manipulating situations or people, they avoid having to show their true feelings or needs, which they may see as weaknesses. This fear of vulnerability can make it difficult for them to form genuine connections, as they are more focused on protecting themselves than on building trust and intimacy.

Manipulators also often seek to avoid responsibility for their actions. By shifting blame, denying wrongdoing, or playing the victim, they can escape accountability and maintain their sense of control. This avoidance of responsibility can be tied to a deep-seated fear of failure or criticism. By manipulating the situation to make it seem like someone else's fault, they protect their fragile ego from the discomfort of admitting mistakes or flaws. This behavior can be particularly damaging in relationships, as it prevents the manipulator from engaging in the honest communication and self-reflection necessary for growth and mutual respect.

Some individuals engage in manipulation out of a desire for power. They may enjoy the feeling of control and superiority that comes from being able to influence others. This desire for power can be rooted in past experiences where they felt powerless or were subjected to manipulation themselves. By becoming the manipulator, they may feel as though they are reclaiming control over their lives. However, this pursuit of power often comes at the expense of others' autonomy and well-being, leading to unhealthy and damaging relationships.

The psychology behind manipulation is complex and multifaceted. It often involves a combination of deep-seated insecurities, a need for control, a lack of empathy, and learned behaviors from past experiences. Manipulators use these tactics to protect themselves, gain validation, avoid responsibility, or achieve their goals, often without regard for the harm they cause to others. Understanding these psychological motivations can help us recognize manipulative behavior and take steps to protect ourselves from its damaging effects. Recognizing the underlying reasons for manipulation can also lead to a deeper understanding of the manipulator's behavior, though it's important to remember that this understanding does not excuse the harm they may cause in a relationship.

CHAPTER 2

The Emotional Effects of Manipulation

Gaslighting and Self-Doubt

Gaslighting is a form of psychological manipulation where the manipulator seeks to make the victim question their own reality, memory, or perceptions. This tactic is insidious because it slowly erodes the victim's sense of self and reality, leading to confusion, self-doubt, and a feeling of being trapped in the relationship. The term "gaslighting" originates from a 1938 play called Gas Light, where a husband manipulates his wife into believing she is going insane by dimming the gaslights in their home and then denying that the lights changed at all. This method of manipulation has become widely recognized as a common tactic used by individuals who want to control and dominate their partners.

Gaslighting begins subtly. The manipulator may start by questioning the victim's memory of specific events. For instance, if the victim recalls a conversation where the manipulator made hurtful comments, the manipulator might respond by saying, "I never said that. You're just imagining things." Over time, the victim begins to doubt their own memory, wondering if they are indeed mistaken or even losing their grip on reality. This doubt is compounded when the manipulator repeatedly denies the truth or twists it in such a way that the victim begins to rely on the manipulator's version of events instead of trusting their own perceptions.

Another common tactic in gaslighting is trivializing the victim's feelings or reactions. For example, if the victim expresses that they feel hurt by something the manipulator did, the manipulator might respond with phrases like, "You're overreacting," or "You're too sensitive." By dismissing the victim's emotions, the manipulator makes the victim feel as though their feelings are invalid or unreasonable. Over time, this can lead the victim to suppress their emotions, second-guess their reactions, and ultimately doubt their own ability to assess situations accurately.

A more extreme form of gaslighting involves the manipulator creating scenarios or altering facts to confuse the victim. For example, the manipulator might move the victim's belongings and then claim that the victim misplaced them. When the victim expresses confusion, the manipulator might suggest that the victim is becoming forgetful or disorganized. In more severe cases, the manipulator may even convince the victim that they are mentally unstable, pushing them to seek help for problems that don't exist. This level of manipulation can have devastating effects on the victim's mental health, leading them to feel isolated, powerless, and dependent on the manipulator for guidance and support.

Gaslighting is particularly harmful because it targets the victim's self-trust. By constantly undermining the victim's perception of reality, the manipulator creates an environment where the victim no longer feels confident in their own judgment. This can lead to a deep sense of insecurity and a loss of self-esteem. The victim may begin to believe that they are incompetent or unworthy of making decisions, which can make them more reliant on the manipulator. This dependency further strengthens the manipulator's control over the victim, making it even more difficult for the victim to recognize the manipulation and break free from the toxic relationship.

The effects of gaslighting extend beyond the individual's relationship with the manipulator. As self-doubt and confusion take hold, the victim may begin to question their interactions with others as well. They might become hesitant to share their thoughts or feelings, fearing that they will be judged or dismissed as they have been in the manipulative relationship. This can lead to social withdrawal, as the victim isolates themselves to avoid the pain of further invalidation. Over time, the victim's world becomes smaller, and their sense of reality becomes increasingly distorted by the manipulator's influence.

In addition to self-doubt, gaslighting can cause a profound sense of confusion. The victim may feel as though they are constantly walking on eggshells, unsure of what is real and what is not. This confusion can be paralyzing, preventing the victim from taking action to address the situation or seek help. They may feel trapped in a state of constant uncertainty, unable to trust their own thoughts, feelings, or perceptions. This mental fog can make it difficult for the victim to see the manipulator's behavior for what it is and recognize the need to protect themselves from further harm.

The psychological impact of gaslighting can be long-lasting. Even after the victim leaves the manipulative relationship, the effects of gaslighting may persist. The victim might continue to struggle with self-doubt, questioning their own judgment in new situations and relationships. They may also have difficulty trusting others, fearing that they will be manipulated or deceived again. This lingering sense of vulnerability can make it challenging for the victim to rebuild their confidence and regain control over their life.

It's important to note that gaslighting doesn't just occur in romantic relationships; it can happen in any type of relationship, including friendships, family dynamics, and professional settings. In all cases, the goal of the manipulator is to undermine the victim's sense of reality in order to exert control over them. Recognizing the signs of gaslighting is the first step in protecting oneself from its damaging effects.

Some common signs of gaslighting include constantly second-guessing yourself, feeling like you're overly sensitive, or frequently apologizing even when you've done nothing wrong. Victims may also find themselves making excuses for the manipulator's behavior or feeling confused about their own thoughts and feelings. If these signs are present, it's crucial to take a step back and evaluate the relationship with a clear mind, possibly seeking input from trusted friends or a mental health professional.

Breaking free from gaslighting requires the victim to reclaim their sense of reality and self-trust. This process can be difficult, especially if the victim has been subjected to gaslighting for an extended period. However, with support and self-awareness, it is possible to overcome the effects of gaslighting and rebuild confidence in one's perceptions and decisions.

Reaching out for help is a critical part of this recovery process. Friends, family, or a therapist can provide the validation and perspective that the victim needs to see the manipulator's behavior for what it is. Therapy can be particularly beneficial in helping the victim rebuild their self-esteem, set healthy boundaries, and develop strategies for recognizing and resisting manipulation in the future.

Gaslighting is a powerful and damaging form of manipulation that can leave victims feeling confused, self-doubting, and disconnected from reality. It operates by undermining the victim's perception of reality and eroding their confidence in their own judgment. The effects of gaslighting can be profound and long-lasting, but with awareness, support, and professional help, victims can reclaim their sense of self and break free from the manipulative influence. Understanding gaslighting and its impact is essential for anyone who may be experiencing or witnessing this form of manipulation, as it provides the foundation for taking action to protect oneself and others from its harmful effects.

Emotional Blackmail

Emotional blackmail is a form of psychological manipulation in which one person uses fear, guilt, and obligation to control another. It's a powerful tool that manipulators use to get what they want by exploiting the emotional vulnerabilities of their partner. This tactic can be subtle or overt, but its core goal is to coerce the victim into complying with the manipulator's demands, often at the expense of the victim's own well-being and desires.

In emotional blackmail, the manipulator often creates a scenario where the victim feels that they must choose between their own needs and the needs of the manipulator. The manipulator presents their demands in such a way that the victim feels immense pressure to comply, usually out of fear of losing the relationship, being punished emotionally, or causing harm to the manipulator. This pressure can be overwhelming, leading the victim to act against their own best interests simply to alleviate the immediate emotional discomfort.

One of the most common techniques of emotional blackmail is the use of guilt. The manipulator might suggest that if the victim truly loved or cared for them, they would comply with their wishes. They may say things like, "If you really loved me, you would do this for me," or "I can't believe you would hurt me like this." These statements are designed to make the victim feel guilty for even considering their own needs or boundaries. The victim may start to believe that they are selfish or unloving if they don't give in to the manipulator's demands, leading them to sacrifice their own happiness to avoid the guilt.

Fear is another powerful tool in emotional blackmail. The manipulator may threaten to end the relationship, harm themselves, or even harm the victim if their demands are not met. For example, a manipulator might say, "If you leave me, I don't know what I'll do. I might hurt myself." This kind of threat creates a deep sense of fear in the victim, who may feel that they have no choice but to comply to prevent something terrible from happening. The fear of losing the relationship or causing harm to the manipulator can be so intense that the victim feels trapped, unable to assert their own needs or boundaries.

Obligation is the third key element of emotional blackmail. The manipulator often plays on the victim's sense of duty or responsibility. They might remind the victim of all the things they have done for them, saying things like, "After everything I've done for you, this is how you repay me?" or "You owe me this." By framing their demands as something the victim is obligated to fulfill, the manipulator makes it difficult for the victim to refuse without feeling like they are being unfair or ungrateful. This sense of obligation can be particularly strong in relationships where there is a significant power imbalance, such as in parent-child relationships or relationships where one partner is financially dependent on the other.

Recognizing emotional blackmail can be challenging because it often plays on emotions that are natural in relationships, such as love, care, and concern. However, there are clear signs that indicate when these emotions are being manipulated for control. For example, if you find yourself constantly compromising your own needs to avoid guilt, fear, or a sense of obligation, you may be experiencing emotional blackmail. Another sign is feeling like you have no choice but to comply with your partner's demands, even when those demands make you uncomfortable or unhappy.

To resist emotional blackmail, it's crucial to develop strong boundaries and a clear sense of your own needs and values. Start by recognizing that your emotions and needs are valid and deserve to be respected. It's important to remember that love and care should not come with conditions that require you to sacrifice your own well-being. If you find that your partner is using guilt, fear, or obligation to control you, take a step back and assess the situation with a clear mind. Ask yourself whether the demands being placed on you are reasonable and whether complying with them aligns with your own values and needs.

One effective strategy for resisting emotional blackmail is to assert your boundaries clearly and calmly. When the manipulator tries to use guilt, fear, or obligation against you, respond by stating your boundaries firmly. For example, you might say, "I understand that you're upset, but I need to take care of myself in this situation," or "I care about you, but I can't do this because it goes against my values." By standing firm in your boundaries, you communicate that while you care about the other person, you are not willing to be controlled through manipulation.

It's also important to seek support from trusted friends, family members, or a therapist who can provide an outside perspective on the situation. Often, victims of emotional blackmail feel isolated and unsure of their own judgment, so having someone to talk to can help clarify what's happening and provide validation for your feelings. A therapist can also help you develop strategies for maintaining your boundaries and building your self-esteem, which is crucial for resisting manipulation.

If the emotional blackmail persists or escalates, it may be necessary to distance yourself from the manipulator or even end the relationship. This can be a difficult and painful decision, especially if the relationship is long-standing or involves deep emotional ties. However, it's important to prioritize your own mental and emotional health. Continuing to stay in a relationship where you are being emotionally manipulated can have serious long-term effects on your self-esteem, mental health, and overall well-being.

Emotional blackmail is a harmful form of manipulation that uses guilt, fear, and obligation to control another person. It can be subtle or overt, but its impact is always damaging to the victim's sense of self and autonomy. Recognizing the signs of emotional blackmail and developing strategies to resist it are crucial steps in protecting yourself from this type of manipulation. By setting strong boundaries, seeking support, and prioritizing your own needs and values, you can break free from the cycle of emotional blackmail and reclaim control over your life.

Codependency and Manipulation

Codependency and manipulation often go hand in hand, creating a complex dynamic where one person's excessive emotional reliance on another makes them more vulnerable to being controlled or manipulated. Codependency is characterized by an unhealthy attachment to another person, where an individual's sense of self-worth and identity becomes deeply intertwined with the approval, needs, and emotions of that person. This excessive reliance can lead to a willingness to do anything to maintain the relationship, even at the expense of one's own well-being.

Individuals who are codependent tend to have an overwhelming need to be needed. They derive their sense of value from taking care of others, often to the point of neglecting their own needs. This self-sacrificing behavior can make them prime targets for manipulators, who are adept at recognizing and exploiting such vulnerabilities. A manipulator might see the codependent's need for approval and use it to their advantage, knowing that the codependent person is likely to go to great lengths to avoid conflict or rejection.

One of the reasons codependent individuals are more susceptible to manipulation is their difficulty in setting and enforcing boundaries. Boundaries are essential in any healthy relationship, as they define what is acceptable behavior and what is not. However, in a codependent relationship, boundaries often become blurred or nonexistent. The codependent person may struggle to say no, even when they are uncomfortable with a situation, because they fear losing the relationship or disappointing the other person. This lack of boundaries creates an environment where a manipulator can easily take control, pushing the codependent person to comply with their demands without resistance.

The fear of abandonment is another significant factor that makes codependent individuals more vulnerable to manipulation. Codependents often have an intense fear of being alone or rejected, which can lead them to tolerate unacceptable behavior in a relationship. A manipulator might use this fear to their advantage by threatening to leave or withdraw their affection if the codependent person does not comply with their wishes. This tactic can be particularly effective, as the codependent's primary goal is often to keep the relationship intact at all costs, even if it means sacrificing their own needs and well-being.

Moreover, codependent individuals often struggle with low self-esteem and a lack of self-worth. They may believe that they are not deserving of love or respect unless they are constantly giving to others. This mindset can make them more willing to endure manipulation, as they may feel that they need to earn the other person's love or approval. A manipulator might exploit this insecurity by making the codependent person feel that they are lucky to have the relationship, or that they must continue to give and sacrifice to maintain it.

In many cases, codependents may also have a history of being in relationships where manipulation was present, either in their family of origin or in past romantic relationships. This history can create a pattern of behavior where they are conditioned to accept manipulation as a normal part of relationships. They may not recognize the signs of manipulation because they have become so accustomed to putting others' needs before their own. As a result, they may be more likely to excuse or overlook manipulative behavior, believing that it is their responsibility to keep the relationship going, no matter what.

The dynamic of a codependent relationship often leads to a cycle of manipulation where the codependent person continually gives and the manipulator continually takes. The more the codependent gives, the more the manipulator demands, creating a situation where the codependent person becomes increasingly depleted and controlled. This cycle can be difficult to break, as the codependent person may not see a way out without losing the relationship, which is their primary source of identity and self-worth.

To break free from this cycle, it is crucial for codependent individuals to develop a stronger sense of self and learn to set healthy boundaries. Building self-esteem and recognizing one's own value outside of the relationship are key steps in this process. It is important for codependents to understand that they deserve to be in a relationship where their needs are met and where they are treated with respect. This realization can empower them to stand up to manipulative behavior and refuse to be controlled by another person's demands.

Therapy can be an invaluable tool for individuals struggling with codependency, as it provides a safe space to explore these issues and develop healthier patterns of relating to others. A therapist can help a codependent person identify the root causes of their behavior, such as childhood experiences or past traumas, and work through these issues in a constructive way. Therapy can also provide practical strategies for setting boundaries, building self-esteem, and resisting manipulation, which are essential skills for breaking free from a codependent relationship.

In addition to therapy, support groups for codependents can offer a sense of community and understanding, helping individuals realize that they are not alone in their struggles. Sharing experiences with others who have faced similar challenges can provide valuable insights and encouragement, as well as practical advice for dealing with manipulation in relationships. These groups can also help codependent individuals see the difference between healthy and unhealthy relationships, reinforcing the importance of self-care and autonomy.

Codependency creates a fertile ground for manipulation by fostering a dynamic where one person's excessive emotional reliance on another makes them more vulnerable to control. The codependent's fear of abandonment, difficulty in setting boundaries, and low self-esteem all contribute to their susceptibility to manipulation. Breaking free from this cycle requires a strong sense of self, the ability to set healthy boundaries, and support from therapy or support groups. By addressing these underlying issues, codependent individuals can learn to protect themselves from manipulation and build healthier, more balanced relationships.

CHAPTER 3

Identifying Your Vulnerabilities

Self-Esteem and Manipulation

Low self-esteem is closely linked to vulnerability to manipulation in relationships. When individuals have low self-esteem, they often struggle with feelings of inadequacy, self-doubt, and a lack of self-worth. These internal struggles can make them more susceptible to being manipulated by others, particularly those who recognize and exploit their insecurities. Understanding this connection is crucial for anyone who wants to protect themselves from manipulation and build healthier, more empowering relationships.

People with low self-esteem often seek validation and approval from others because they do not believe in their own intrinsic value. This need for external validation can make them easy targets for manipulators, who may offer praise, attention, or affection as a way to control them. For example, a manipulator might shower a person with compliments or kindness to gain their trust and then use that trust to influence their decisions. The individual with low self-esteem, hungry for validation, might go along with the manipulator's wishes, even when it goes against their own best interests.

This cycle of seeking approval and being manipulated can reinforce feelings of low self-worth. Each time the individual compromises their own needs or values to please the manipulator, they may feel weaker and more dependent on the manipulator's approval. Over time, this can lead to a sense of helplessness, where the individual feels they are unable to make decisions or take action without the manipulator's input or guidance. This dependency can make it even more challenging to break free from the manipulative relationship.

One of the reasons low self-esteem makes individuals more vulnerable to manipulation is that they often have difficulty setting and enforcing boundaries. Boundaries are essential for maintaining a sense of self and protecting one's emotional and psychological well-being in relationships. However, individuals with low self-esteem may fear that setting boundaries will lead to rejection or conflict, so they may avoid asserting their needs or saying no. This fear of confrontation can be easily exploited by a manipulator, who may push the individual to do things they are uncomfortable with, knowing that they are unlikely to resist.

Moreover, people with low self-esteem often internalize negative messages from others, which can further erode their sense of self-worth. A manipulator might criticize or belittle the individual, subtly or overtly, to make them feel unworthy or inadequate. These negative messages can become internalized, leading the individual to believe that they are not good enough or deserving of respect. This self-criticism can create a downward spiral, where the individual becomes more reliant on the manipulator for validation, while also feeling increasingly powerless and trapped.

Protecting oneself from manipulation when struggling with low self-esteem requires a multifaceted approach that focuses on building self-worth, developing strong boundaries, and cultivating self-awareness. One of the first steps in this process is recognizing the negative thought patterns and beliefs that contribute to low self-esteem. This might involve examining the origins of these beliefs, such as childhood experiences, past relationships, or societal pressures, and challenging their validity. By questioning these negative beliefs, individuals can begin to replace them with more positive and empowering self-perceptions.

Building self-esteem also involves learning to validate oneself, rather than relying on others for approval. This means recognizing and appreciating one's own strengths, achievements, and qualities, regardless of whether others acknowledge them. Practicing self-compassion is a key component of this process, as it involves treating oneself with kindness and understanding, especially in moments of failure or self-doubt. By cultivating a positive and supportive inner dialogue, individuals can strengthen their sense of self-worth and reduce their reliance on external validation.

Developing strong boundaries is another crucial aspect of protecting oneself from manipulation. This involves clearly defining what behaviors are acceptable and unacceptable in relationships, and being willing to enforce these boundaries when necessary. For individuals with low self-esteem, setting boundaries can be challenging, as it may feel uncomfortable or risky to assert their needs. However, practicing boundary-setting in small, manageable steps can help build confidence and reinforce the importance of self-respect.

In addition to setting boundaries, it is important to recognize and resist the tactics used by manipulators. This might involve becoming more attuned to manipulative behaviors, such as guilt-tripping, gaslighting, or emotional blackmail, and learning to identify when these tactics are being used. Developing this awareness can empower individuals to respond more assertively and to refuse to be controlled by these manipulative tactics. It can also help them to recognize when a relationship is unhealthy and to take steps to protect themselves, whether that means seeking support, distancing themselves from the manipulator, or ending the relationship altogether.

Seeking support from trusted friends, family members, or a therapist can also be invaluable for individuals with low self-esteem. Supportive relationships can provide a safe space for individuals to express their feelings, gain perspective, and receive encouragement. A therapist, in particular, can help individuals explore the underlying issues that contribute to low self-esteem and develop strategies for building self-worth and resilience. Therapy can also offer practical tools for managing relationships and protecting oneself from manipulation, such as assertiveness training, cognitive-behavioral techniques, and mindfulness practices.

The link between low self-esteem and vulnerability to manipulation is rooted in the individual's need for external validation, difficulty setting boundaries, and susceptibility to internalizing negative messages. To protect themselves from manipulation, individuals with low self-esteem must focus on building self-worth, developing strong boundaries, and cultivating self-awareness. By recognizing and challenging negative thought patterns, practicing self-compassion, and seeking support, they can strengthen their sense of self and reduce their vulnerability to manipulation. Ultimately, this process of self-empowerment can lead to healthier, more balanced relationships where their needs and boundaries are respected.

Unresolved Trauma and Its Role

Unresolved trauma from the past can significantly increase an individual's vulnerability to manipulation in relationships. Trauma, whether from childhood experiences, past relationships, or other life events, can leave deep emotional scars that affect how a person perceives themselves and others. When these traumatic experiences are not fully processed or healed, they can create patterns of behavior and thinking that make a person more susceptible to being manipulated. Understanding the connection between unresolved trauma and manipulation is essential for those seeking to protect themselves and foster healthier relationships.

Trauma often results in feelings of fear, shame, guilt, and helplessness. These emotions can persist long after the traumatic event has occurred, influencing a person's self-esteem, trust in others, and overall sense of security. For someone who has experienced trauma, especially in a close relationship, it can be difficult to feel safe and secure in subsequent relationships. The lingering effects of trauma can cause individuals to question their worth and to fear rejection, abandonment, or conflict. These fears can make them more likely to tolerate unhealthy behaviors, including manipulation, in an attempt to avoid triggering their unresolved emotional pain.

One way trauma influences vulnerability to manipulation is through the development of maladaptive coping mechanisms. For example, someone who has experienced abuse or neglect in the past may have learned to suppress their own needs and emotions as a way to avoid further harm. This can manifest in current relationships as a tendency to prioritize the needs of others over their own, even when doing so is detrimental to their well-being. A manipulator can easily exploit this tendency, using guilt, pity, or obligation to control the person's actions and decisions.

Additionally, unresolved trauma can lead to a heightened state of emotional reactivity. Traumatic experiences can leave a person feeling constantly on edge, as if they are in a state of perpetual threat. This hypervigilance can make it difficult to think clearly or to recognize when they are being manipulated. Manipulators may use this emotional sensitivity to their advantage, deliberately provoking the person or playing on their fears to manipulate their behavior. For instance, a manipulator might create situations that trigger the person's trauma responses, such as abandonment anxiety or fear of conflict, in order to exert control over them.

Another way unresolved trauma contributes to susceptibility to manipulation is through the formation of negative self-beliefs. Trauma can distort a person's self-image, leading them to believe that they are unworthy of love, respect, or care. These beliefs can make them more likely to accept mistreatment or manipulation in relationships because they feel they do not deserve better. A manipulator might reinforce these negative self-beliefs by criticizing, belittling, or gaslighting the person, making them feel even more powerless and dependent on the manipulator's approval.

Healing from past trauma is a crucial step in reducing vulnerability to manipulation. The process of healing involves acknowledging the trauma, understanding its impact, and working through the associated emotions and beliefs. One of the first steps in this process is recognizing the ways in which the trauma has affected one's current behavior and relationships. This might involve identifying patterns of people-pleasing, avoidance, or emotional reactivity that have developed as a result of the trauma. By becoming aware of these patterns, individuals can begin to challenge them and make conscious choices that support their well-being.

Therapy can be an essential tool for healing from trauma. A trained therapist can provide a safe and supportive environment for individuals to explore their trauma, process their emotions, and develop healthier coping mechanisms. Different therapeutic approaches, such as cognitive-behavioral therapy, eye movement desensitization and reprocessing, or trauma-focused therapy, can be effective in helping individuals heal from trauma. These therapies can help individuals reframe negative self-beliefs, manage emotional triggers, and build resilience against future manipulation.

In addition to therapy, self-care practices can play a vital role in healing from trauma. Self-care involves taking steps to nurture one's physical, emotional, and mental health. This might include engaging in regular exercise, practicing mindfulness or meditation, maintaining a balanced diet, and ensuring adequate rest. Self-care also involves setting boundaries and prioritizing one's own needs and well-being in relationships. For someone with unresolved trauma, learning to say no, to ask for what they need, and to protect their emotional space can be empowering steps toward healing and self-empowerment.

Building a strong support network is another important aspect of healing from trauma. Surrounding oneself with supportive friends, family members, or community groups can provide a sense of safety and connection. Supportive relationships can offer validation, encouragement, and understanding, which are crucial for rebuilding self-esteem and trust in others. In contrast, isolating oneself or remaining in toxic relationships can reinforce feelings of helplessness and make it more difficult to heal from trauma.

Practicing self-compassion is also essential in the healing process. Trauma survivors often carry feelings of guilt, shame, or self-blame, believing that they are somehow responsible for the trauma they experienced. Self-compassion involves treating oneself with kindness and understanding, recognizing that the trauma was not their fault, and that they deserve healing and happiness. By practicing self-compassion, individuals can begin to let go of negative self-beliefs and embrace a more positive and empowering self-image.

It is important to recognize that healing from trauma is a journey, not a destination. It takes time, patience, and perseverance to work through the deep emotional wounds that trauma can leave behind. There may be setbacks or moments of doubt along the way, but each step forward is a step toward greater self-awareness, self-worth, and resilience. As individuals heal from trauma, they can develop a stronger sense of self and become more equipped to protect themselves from manipulation in future relationships.

Unresolved trauma from the past can make individuals more susceptible to manipulation by affecting their self-esteem, emotional reactivity, and coping mechanisms. However, by acknowledging and healing from this trauma, individuals can build resilience, develop healthier relationships, and protect themselves from manipulation. Therapy, self-care, support networks, and self-compassion are all important tools in the healing process. Through this journey of healing, individuals can reclaim their sense of self-worth and create relationships that are based on mutual respect, trust, and care.

Setting Boundaries

Setting boundaries in relationships is crucial for protecting oneself from manipulation and maintaining a sense of self-respect and autonomy. Boundaries are the limits we set in our interactions with others to ensure that our values, needs, and feelings are respected. They are essential for healthy relationships, as they help define what is acceptable and unacceptable behavior, allowing both partners to understand each other's expectations and maintain a sense of mutual respect. Without clear boundaries, relationships can become unbalanced, with one person exerting control over the other, leading to manipulation and emotional harm.

The importance of setting boundaries cannot be overstated. Boundaries serve as a protective barrier against manipulation by clearly defining what behaviors are acceptable and what will not be tolerated. When boundaries are well-defined and communicated, they help prevent others from taking advantage of our vulnerabilities. Manipulators often seek out individuals with weak or poorly enforced boundaries because it allows them to exert control more easily. By establishing strong boundaries, individuals can protect themselves from being coerced, guilt-tripped, or emotionally blackmailed into actions or decisions that are not in their best interest.

Boundaries also play a critical role in maintaining a healthy sense of self. When boundaries are respected, individuals feel valued, respected, and understood in their relationships. This contributes to a positive self-image and emotional well-being. On the other hand, when boundaries are violated, it can lead to feelings of frustration, resentment, and a loss of self-worth. Over time, repeated boundary violations can erode a person's confidence and self-esteem, making them more susceptible to further manipulation. Therefore, setting and maintaining boundaries is essential for preserving one's self-respect and emotional health.

Effective boundaries are specific, clear, and consistent. They are communicated directly and assertively, leaving no room for misunderstanding or ambiguity. For example, an effective boundary in a relationship might involve setting limits on how much time and energy one is willing to invest in certain activities or interactions. If a partner frequently demands attention or time that interferes with other important aspects of life, such as work, hobbies, or self-care, it is important to communicate this boundary clearly. An example of setting this boundary might be, "I value our time together, but I also need time for myself and my responsibilities. I can spend time with you on the weekends, but during the week, I need to focus on my work and personal interests."

Another example of an effective boundary is related to communication and emotional expression. In a healthy relationship, both partners should feel free to express their thoughts and emotions without fear of judgment or retaliation. However, if one partner frequently dismisses or invalidates the other's feelings, it may be necessary to set a boundary around how emotions are communicated. An example of this boundary might be, "I understand that we may not always agree, but it's important to me that my feelings are acknowledged and respected. I need us to have conversations where we listen to each other without interrupting or dismissing each other's feelings."

Boundaries can also be set around physical and emotional space. For instance, if a partner frequently invades one's personal space or demands constant attention, it is important to establish a boundary to protect one's sense of autonomy. An example of this boundary might be, "I appreciate that you care about spending time together, but I also need time alone to recharge. I need you to respect my personal space and allow me some time each day to be by myself."

In addition to setting boundaries, it is equally important to enforce them consistently. Manipulators often test boundaries to see if they can be pushed or ignored. If a boundary is not enforced, it sends a message that the behavior is acceptable, which can lead to further manipulation. Therefore, it is essential to follow through with the consequences if a boundary is violated. For example, if a partner repeatedly disrespects a boundary around personal space, the consequence might be taking a temporary break from the relationship to reestablish the boundary. Enforcing boundaries requires assertiveness and confidence, but it is a necessary step in protecting oneself from manipulation.

It is important to recognize that setting boundaries is not about being rigid or controlling; rather, it is about creating a healthy balance between one's own needs and the needs of the relationship. Boundaries should be flexible enough to allow for growth and change in the relationship but firm enough to protect one's well-being. Effective communication is key to achieving this balance. When setting boundaries, it is important to express them in a way that is respectful and considerate of the other person's feelings. For example, instead of saying, "You always ignore my feelings, and I can't stand it," a more effective approach might be, "I feel hurt when my feelings are not acknowledged. I need us to work on being more supportive of each other's emotions."

In relationships, boundaries should be mutually agreed upon and respected by both partners. It is not only important to set personal boundaries but also to understand and respect the boundaries set by the other person. This mutual respect fosters trust, understanding, and cooperation in the relationship. When both partners are aware of each other's boundaries and make an effort to honor them, it creates a safe and supportive environment where both individuals can thrive.

It is also worth noting that setting boundaries is an ongoing process. As relationships evolve, so do the needs and expectations of the individuals involved. Therefore, it is important to regularly reassess and adjust boundaries as needed. Open and honest communication is essential for this process. If a boundary needs to be changed or updated, it is important to have a conversation with the partner to discuss the reasons for the change and to come to a mutual agreement.

Setting and maintaining boundaries in relationships is essential for protecting against manipulation and preserving one's sense of self-respect and autonomy. Boundaries define what behaviors are acceptable and help prevent others from taking advantage of our vulnerabilities. Effective boundaries are specific, clear, and consistently enforced, and they should be communicated in a respectful and assertive manner. By setting strong boundaries, individuals can create healthier, more balanced relationships where both partners feel valued and respected.

CHAPTER 4

Understanding the Manipulator's Playbook

Tactics of Control

Manipulators often employ a range of tactics to control their partners, exerting influence in subtle and overt ways. These tactics are designed to undermine the other person's autonomy, create dependency, and maintain the manipulator's power within the relationship. Understanding these tactics is essential for recognizing when manipulation is taking place and for developing strategies to counteract it.

One of the most common tactics of control is isolation. Manipulators often work to cut off their partners from friends, family, and other support systems. This isolation can be achieved through various means, such as discouraging social interactions, creating conflicts between the partner and their loved ones, or monopolizing their time to prevent them from maintaining outside relationships. The goal of isolation is to make the partner more reliant on the manipulator for emotional and social needs, thus increasing the manipulator's control over them. For example, a manipulator might say, "Your friends don't really care about you like I do," or "Why do you need to spend time with them when you have me?" These statements are designed to make the partner feel guilty for wanting to maintain other relationships, leading them to withdraw from their social circle.

Guilt-tripping is another powerful tactic used by manipulators to control their partners. By inducing feelings of guilt, the manipulator can influence their partner's behavior to align with their own desires. Guilt-tripping often involves making the partner feel responsible for the manipulator's emotions or well-being. For instance, a manipulator might say,

"If you loved me, you would do this for me," or "I can't believe you would hurt me like this after everything I've done for you." These statements are intended to make the partner feel guilty for not complying with the manipulator's demands, even if those demands are unreasonable or harmful. Over time, this tactic can lead the partner to prioritize the manipulator's needs and desires over their own, eroding their sense of self and autonomy.

Intimidation is a more overt tactic of control that involves using fear to dominate the partner. This fear can be physical, emotional, or psychological. Physical intimidation might involve threats of violence or aggressive behavior, such as shouting, throwing objects, or making menacing gestures. Emotional and psychological intimidation, on the other hand, can be more subtle but equally damaging. This might include threats of self-harm, withdrawal of affection, or making the partner feel worthless and incapable. For example, a manipulator might say, "If you leave me, I'll hurt myself," or "No one else would ever want you." These tactics are designed to make the partner feel trapped in the relationship, afraid to leave or assert their own needs.

Another tactic used by manipulators is gaslighting, which involves distorting reality to make the partner doubt their own perceptions and sanity. The manipulator may deny things they have said or done, twist the truth, or accuse the partner of being overly sensitive or irrational. For instance, if the partner confronts the manipulator about hurtful behavior, the manipulator might respond with, "You're imagining things," or "You're just being paranoid." Over time, gaslighting can lead the partner to question their own memory, judgment, and reality, making them more dependent on the manipulator's version of events.

Love-bombing is a tactic where the manipulator overwhelms their partner with excessive affection, attention, and flattery in the early stages of the relationship. This creates an intense emotional connection and makes the partner feel special and valued. However, once the partner is emotionally invested, the manipulator may withdraw this affection and begin to exert control. The sudden shift can leave the partner confused and desperate to regain the manipulator's approval, making them more susceptible to manipulation. For example, a manipulator might shower their partner with gifts, compliments, and constant attention, only to become distant and critical once they feel secure in the relationship.

Manipulators also use triangulation as a tactic of control, involving third parties to create jealousy, competition, or insecurity in the partner. This can be done by flirting with others, comparing the partner to someone else, or bringing up past relationships. The goal is to make the partner feel insecure and more dependent on the manipulator for validation. For instance, a manipulator might say, "My ex used to do this for me, why can't you?" or "So-and-so is really attractive; maybe I made the wrong choice." These statements are intended to make the partner feel inadequate and desperate to prove their worth.

Financial control is another common tactic used by manipulators to exert power over their partners. This can involve controlling access to money, dictating how the partner spends their finances, or deliberately creating financial dependency. For example, a manipulator might insist on managing all the finances, giving the partner an allowance, or preventing them from working. This financial control can make it difficult for the partner to leave the relationship, as they may feel they have no means to support themselves independently.

Silent treatment is a passive-aggressive tactic where the manipulator withholds communication or affection as a way to punish or control their partner. By refusing to speak or engage, the manipulator creates a sense of uncertainty and anxiety in the partner, who may feel compelled to apologize or give in to the manipulator's demands in order to restore harmony. The silent treatment can be particularly effective because it taps into the partner's fear of abandonment or rejection, making them more likely to conform to the manipulator's wishes.

Emotional manipulation often involves playing the victim to elicit sympathy and guilt from the partner. The manipulator may exaggerate their own suffering, blame others for their problems, or portray themselves as helpless and in need of rescue. By doing so, they shift the focus away from their own behavior and place the burden of responsibility on the partner. For instance, a manipulator might say, "I've had such a hard life, you should understand why I act this way," or "I can't cope without you." This tactic is designed to make the partner feel obligated to support and care for the manipulator, even at the expense of their own well-being.

The tactics of control used by manipulators in relationships are varied and can be both subtle and overt. These tactics, such as isolation, guilt-tripping, intimidation, gaslighting, love-bombing, triangulation, financial control, silent treatment, and emotional manipulation, are all designed to undermine the partner's autonomy, create dependency, and maintain the manipulator's power. Recognizing these tactics is the first step in protecting oneself from manipulation and taking back control of one's life. Understanding how these tactics work and the impact they have on the victim can empower individuals to set boundaries, seek support, and ultimately break free from the cycle of manipulation.

Twisting the Narrative

Manipulators often use the tactic of twisting the narrative to gain control in a relationship. This involves altering the truth by using lies, half-truths, or selective omissions to shape the story in their favor. By controlling the narrative, they can shift blame, avoid accountability, and create confusion, leaving their partner uncertain about what is real and what is not.

One of the most common ways manipulators twist the narrative is through outright lies. These lies can range from small, seemingly insignificant fabrications to large, life-altering deceptions. The purpose of these lies is to distort the reality of the situation, making it difficult for the partner to discern the truth. For instance, a manipulator might lie about where they were or who they were with to avoid confrontation or to cover up behavior they know would be unacceptable to their partner. Over time, these lies accumulate, creating a false version of events that the partner may begin to believe, especially if they are constantly reassured by the manipulator.

Half-truths are another method manipulators use to twist the narrative. A half-truth is a statement that is partially true but misleading because it leaves out important details or presents the truth in a way that skews its meaning. By presenting only part of the truth, the manipulator can create a narrative that supports their agenda while hiding the full reality of the situation. For example, a manipulator might admit to speaking to an ex-partner but leave out the fact that the conversation was flirtatious or inappropriate. By doing so, they can claim honesty while still keeping their partner in the dark about the true nature of their actions.

Selective omission, where a manipulator deliberately leaves out critical information, is another way to twist the narrative. This tactic allows the manipulator to control what their partner knows, shaping their perception of events. By omitting certain facts, the manipulator can avoid difficult conversations, deflect blame, or create a version of reality that is more favorable to them. For instance, if a partner asks about a problem at work, the manipulator might choose to omit details that would reveal their own mistakes, instead portraying themselves as a victim of circumstances. This selective sharing of information creates a skewed narrative that manipulates the partner's understanding of the situation.

Manipulators also twist the narrative by reframing events to make themselves appear in a more positive light while casting their partner in a negative role. This reframing often involves shifting blame onto the partner, making them feel responsible for problems in the relationship. For example, if a manipulator is confronted about hurtful behavior, they might turn the situation around by accusing their partner of being too sensitive or overreacting. By doing this, the manipulator diverts attention away from their own actions and places the burden of guilt on their partner. This tactic not only shifts blame but also erodes the partner's confidence in their own perceptions and feelings.

In addition to reframing events, manipulators may use gaslighting as a way to twist the narrative further. Gaslighting involves denying or distorting reality to make the partner question their own memory, judgment, and sanity. A manipulator might insist that something never happened, even when it clearly did, or claim that the partner is misremembering events. Over time, this can lead the partner to doubt their own ability to recall the truth, making them more reliant on the manipulator's version of events. For instance, a manipulator might say, "I never said that; you're imagining things," or "You're just being paranoid; that's not how it happened." These statements are designed to confuse the partner and make them doubt their own experiences.

Another way manipulators twist the narrative is by playing the victim. By portraying themselves as the wronged party, they can elicit sympathy from their partner while deflecting responsibility for their own actions. This tactic is particularly effective because it shifts the focus away from the manipulator's behavior and onto the partner's supposed wrongdoing. For example, a manipulator might say, "I can't believe you would accuse me of that after everything I've done for you," or "You're hurting me by not trusting me." By casting themselves as the victim, the manipulator can make their partner feel guilty for questioning them, even when those questions are justified.

Manipulators also twist the narrative by exploiting their partner's insecurities. They may exaggerate or fabricate flaws in their partner to create doubt and dependency. For instance, a manipulator might repeatedly tell their partner that they are unattractive, unintelligent, or unlovable, even if these things are untrue. By doing so, the manipulator undermines their partner's self-esteem, making them more likely to believe the distorted narrative the manipulator is creating. This tactic not only shifts blame away from the manipulator but also makes the partner feel unworthy, less likely to challenge the manipulator's behavior, and more dependent on the manipulator for validation.

In some cases, manipulators will use triangulation as a way to twist the narrative further. Triangulation involves bringing in a third party, such as a friend, family member, or even a stranger, to reinforce the manipulator's version of events. By involving others, the manipulator can create the illusion of consensus, making their partner feel isolated and more likely to doubt their own perspective. For example, a manipulator might say, "Even so-and-so agrees with me that you're being unreasonable," or "Everyone else thinks I'm right." This tactic adds an additional layer of pressure on the partner to accept the manipulated narrative.

Manipulators may twist the narrative by projecting their own faults onto their partner. Projection involves accusing the partner of the very behaviors or attitudes that the manipulator themselves is guilty of. This not only deflects blame but also creates confusion and defensiveness in the partner, who may feel compelled to prove their innocence. For instance, if a manipulator is unfaithful, they might accuse their partner of being untrustworthy or overly flirtatious. By projecting their own actions onto their partner, the manipulator shifts attention away from their own wrongdoing and places the partner on the defensive.

Twisting the narrative is a powerful tactic in the manipulator's playbook. Through lies, half-truths, omissions, reframing, gaslighting, playing the victim, exploiting insecurities, triangulation, and projection, manipulators can create a distorted version of reality that serves their interests while undermining their partner's sense of truth and self-worth. Understanding these tactics is crucial for anyone in a relationship with a manipulator, as it allows them to recognize when the narrative is being manipulated and take steps to reclaim their own perspective and truth.

The Cycle of Abuse

The cycle of abuse in manipulative relationships is a repetitive pattern that perpetuates the power and control dynamics between the abuser and the victim. Understanding this cycle is essential in recognizing why individuals often find themselves trapped in abusive relationships despite the harm they endure. The cycle consists of four phases: tension-building, incident, reconciliation, and calm. Each phase serves a particular function in maintaining the abusive relationship and making it difficult for the victim to break free.

The first phase, tension-building, is characterized by increasing strain and stress within the relationship. During this stage, the abuser may become irritable, moody, or unpredictable, creating an atmosphere of anxiety and unease. The victim often feels as though they are walking on eggshells, trying to avoid triggering the abuser's anger or frustration. The tension may manifest through passive-aggressive behavior, such as sarcasm, silent treatment, or subtle put-downs, or it may be more overt, such as criticizing, blaming, or threatening the victim. The abuser's behavior is typically designed to provoke fear and uncertainty, keeping the victim in a state of heightened alertness and emotional distress.

The tension-building phase is crucial in the cycle because it sets the stage for the next phase: the incident. The incident phase is when the abuse becomes explicit and overt. This can take many forms, including verbal, emotional, physical, or sexual abuse. During this phase, the abuser unleashes their anger, frustration, or need for control on the victim, often in a sudden and explosive manner. The incident might involve yelling, name-calling, hitting, or other forms of violence. In some cases, the abuse may be more subtle, such as manipulation, gaslighting, or emotional blackmail. Regardless of the form it takes, the abuse serves to reinforce the abuser's power over the victim and deepen the victim's sense of helplessness and fear.

Following the incident, the relationship typically enters the reconciliation phase, also known as the honeymoon phase. During this stage, the abuser may apologize, express remorse, and make promises to change their behavior. They may shower the victim with affection, gifts, or attention, creating a temporary sense of relief and hope for the future. The abuser's behavior during this phase can be highly manipulative, as they often use their charm and persuasive abilities to convince the victim that the abuse was a one-time occurrence or that it was somehow the victim's fault. The victim, desperate for the relationship to return to a state of normalcy, may accept the abuser's apologies and believe that the situation will improve.

The reconciliation phase is particularly insidious because it creates a sense of emotional dependency in the victim. The contrast between the abuser's loving behavior during this phase and their abusive behavior during the incident phase can be confusing and disorienting for the victim. The victim may cling to the hope that the abuser's promises of change are genuine and that the relationship can return to a happier, more stable state. This hope is often reinforced by the abuser's charm and manipulative tactics, which can make it difficult for the victim to recognize the cyclical nature of the abuse.

The final phase of the cycle is the calm phase, sometimes referred to as the "honeymoon" or "lull" period. During this stage, the relationship appears to return to normalcy. The abuser may be on their best behavior, acting kind, attentive, and caring. The victim may feel a sense of relief and begin to believe that the worst is over. This period of calm can last for varying lengths of time, from days to months, depending on the dynamics of the relationship. However, this phase is deceptive because it is only temporary. The underlying issues of power and control that drive the cycle of abuse have not been resolved, and the cycle is likely to repeat.

The calm phase serves as a trap for the victim, lulling them into a false sense of security. The abuser's seemingly positive behavior during this time reinforces the victim's hope that the relationship can change for the better, making it harder for the victim to leave. The victim may also feel guilty for considering leaving the relationship, especially if the abuser is behaving well during this phase. This guilt, combined with the emotional and psychological manipulation that has occurred throughout the cycle, can create a powerful barrier to the victim's ability to recognize the need for change and to take action to protect themselves.

The repetition of the cycle of abuse is driven by the abuser's need for control and the dynamics of power within the relationship. Each phase of the cycle serves to reinforce the abuser's dominance and the victim's submission. The tension-building phase keeps the victim on edge, the incident phase asserts the abuser's power, the reconciliation phase draws the victim back in, and the calm phase creates a temporary illusion of stability. This cyclical pattern can become deeply ingrained in the relationship, making it difficult for the victim to break free.

Moreover, the cycle of abuse is often reinforced by external factors, such as societal norms, financial dependency, and isolation. Victims of abuse may feel trapped by their circumstances, fearing the consequences of leaving the relationship, such as losing financial support, custody of children, or social standing. Abusers often exploit these vulnerabilities, using them as additional tools of control. The cycle of abuse can also be perpetuated by the victim's own psychological state, including feelings of low self-worth, fear of the unknown, and the emotional trauma caused by the abuse itself.

Understanding the cycle of abuse is critical for both victims and those who support them. Recognizing the pattern can help victims identify the signs of abuse and take steps to protect themselves. It is also important for friends, family members, and professionals to be aware of the cycle so they can offer appropriate support and interventions. Breaking the cycle of abuse requires a combination of awareness, support, and action. Victims need to recognize the pattern of abuse, seek help, and take steps to create a safe and healthy environment for themselves.

The cycle of abuse is a destructive and repetitive pattern that traps victims in a cycle of fear, hope, and despair. Each phase of the cycle serves to reinforce the abuser's control over the victim, making it difficult for the victim to break free. Understanding the dynamics of this cycle is essential for anyone seeking to escape an abusive relationship or support someone who is experiencing abuse. By recognizing the signs of the cycle and taking proactive steps, victims can begin the journey toward healing and freedom.

CHAPTER 5

Breaking Free from Manipulation

Developing Self-Awareness

Developing self-awareness is a powerful tool in recognizing and breaking free from manipulation in relationships. Self-awareness involves having a clear and honest understanding of your own thoughts, feelings, and behaviors, as well as how they interact with others. When individuals are self-aware, they can better identify when they are being manipulated, set appropriate boundaries, and make healthier decisions for their well-being. The process of developing self-awareness requires mindfulness, self-reflection, and a commitment to personal growth.

Mindfulness is a key component of self-awareness. It involves paying attention to your present thoughts and feelings without judgment, allowing you to observe your experiences as they unfold. In the context of relationships, mindfulness can help you notice subtle changes in your emotions, physical sensations, and reactions when interacting with others. For example, if you feel a sense of discomfort, anxiety, or confusion after a conversation with a partner, mindfulness allows you to recognize these feelings as potential indicators of manipulation. By being fully present in your interactions, you can become more attuned to how certain behaviors or words make you feel, which is the first step in identifying manipulation.

Self-reflection is another crucial aspect of developing self-awareness. This involves taking the time to think deeply about your experiences, emotions, and responses. It's about asking yourself important questions: How did that conversation make me feel? Why did I react the way I did? Is there a pattern in how I'm treated in this relationship? Through self-reflection, you can uncover insights into your own vulnerabilities and how they may be exploited by a manipulator. For instance, if you often find yourself feeling guilty or obligated after interactions with your partner, reflecting on these feelings can help you understand if emotional blackmail is at play. Regular self-reflection helps you see the bigger picture of your relationship dynamics and recognize when something is amiss.

One effective strategy for developing self-awareness is journaling. Keeping a journal allows you to document your thoughts, feelings, and experiences on a daily basis. Over time, patterns may emerge that reveal how manipulation is affecting you. Journaling can be particularly helpful in relationships where manipulation is subtle and difficult to detect. By writing down specific incidents, how you felt, and how you responded, you can start to see the ways in which you may be manipulated. This process not only helps you become more aware of manipulation but also empowers you to make changes based on your observations.

Another important aspect of self-awareness is understanding your own values, needs, and boundaries. When you have a clear sense of what you stand for and what you need from a relationship, it becomes easier to recognize when those needs are not being met or when your boundaries are being violated. Manipulators often target individuals who are unsure of their own values or who have difficulty asserting their needs. By developing a strong sense of self, you can resist attempts to undermine your confidence or make you doubt your worth. Take time to define your core values; what is most important to you in a relationship? What are your non-negotiables? Knowing the answers to these questions helps you stay grounded and less susceptible to manipulation.

Building self-awareness also involves becoming familiar with the tactics that manipulators use. Educating yourself about common manipulation techniques, such as gaslighting, guilt-tripping, and emotional blackmail, can help you recognize when these tactics are being used against you. For example, if you notice that your partner frequently makes you question your own memory or perceptions, you may be experiencing gaslighting. Understanding these tactics gives you the knowledge needed to identify manipulation and take steps to protect yourself.

In addition to mindfulness and self-reflection, seeking feedback from trusted friends or a therapist can also enhance your self-awareness. Sometimes, it's difficult to see manipulation clearly when you're in the midst of it. An outside perspective can provide valuable insights that you may not have considered. Trusted friends or a therapist can help you explore your feelings, validate your experiences, and offer guidance on how to navigate the situation. They can also help you identify blind spots; areas where you may be particularly vulnerable to manipulation and develop strategies to strengthen those areas.

One of the challenges in developing self-awareness is the tendency to ignore or rationalize red flags in a relationship. It's common for individuals to downplay or dismiss their own feelings of discomfort, especially when they care deeply about their partner. However, true self-awareness requires honesty with yourself. This means acknowledging when something doesn't feel right and giving yourself permission to explore those feelings. It's important to trust your intuition; if something feels off, it likely is. Being honest with yourself about your feelings and experiences is a critical step in protecting yourself from manipulation.

Developing self-awareness also involves practicing self-compassion. It's easy to be hard on yourself when you realize you've been manipulated, but self-compassion allows you to approach the situation with kindness and understanding. Recognize that everyone has vulnerabilities, and being manipulated does not mean you are weak or flawed. Instead of blaming yourself, focus on what you can learn from the experience and how you can grow stronger moving forward. Self-compassion also helps you set and maintain healthy boundaries, as it reinforces the belief that you deserve to be treated with respect and care.

As you develop self-awareness, it's important to take action based on what you learn. Recognizing manipulation is only the first step; the next step is deciding how to respond. This may involve setting boundaries, seeking support, or even leaving the relationship if necessary. Self-awareness empowers you to make informed decisions that prioritize your well-being. It also helps you build resilience, so you can better navigate challenges and protect yourself from future manipulation.

Developing self-awareness is a crucial skill in recognizing and breaking free from manipulation in relationships. Through mindfulness, self-reflection, journaling, and seeking feedback, you can become more attuned to your own experiences and recognize when manipulation is occurring. Understanding your own values, needs, and boundaries strengthens your ability to resist manipulation and make healthier choices. By practicing self-compassion and taking action based on your self-awareness, you can create a more fulfilling and authentic life, free from the control of manipulators.

Reclaiming Your Power

Reclaiming your power in a relationship with a manipulator is an essential step towards regaining your sense of autonomy, self-worth, and emotional well-being. When someone manipulates you, they exert control over your thoughts, feelings, and actions, often leaving you feeling powerless and confused. However, by taking deliberate steps to set boundaries, assert your needs, and make independent decisions, you can reclaim your power and create a healthier dynamic in your relationship.

The first step in reclaiming your power is recognizing that you have the right to assert your boundaries. Boundaries are the limits you set to protect your physical, emotional, and mental well-being. They define what is acceptable behavior from others and what is not. In relationships with manipulators, boundaries are often blurred or violated, leading to a loss of personal autonomy. Reclaiming your power begins with clearly identifying and communicating your boundaries to your partner. For example, if your partner frequently dismisses your feelings or opinions, you can set a boundary by stating, "I need my feelings to be respected and heard in this relationship. It's important to me that we both listen to each other without judgment."

Once you have established your boundaries, it is crucial to enforce them consistently. This means standing firm when your boundaries are challenged or violated. Manipulators often test boundaries to see if they can push them, but by remaining resolute, you send a clear message that your limits are non-negotiable. Enforcing boundaries may involve saying no to unreasonable requests, refusing to engage in manipulative tactics, or walking away from situations that make you uncomfortable. It's important to remember that enforcing boundaries is not about controlling the other person, but rather about protecting your own well-being.

Another important aspect of reclaiming your power is making decisions independently. Manipulators often undermine their partner's ability to make decisions by creating doubt, fear, or confusion. They may pressure you into making choices that benefit them while disregarding your own needs and desires. To reclaim your power, it is essential to take back control of your decision-making process.

Start by trusting your own judgment and instincts. When faced with a decision, take the time to consider what you truly want and need, rather than what your partner might expect or demand. This might involve weighing the pros and cons, seeking advice from trusted friends or family, or simply giving yourself the space to think things through without external pressure.

As you make decisions independently, it's important to practice self-advocacy. Self-advocacy means standing up for your own needs, rights, and interests in the relationship. This involves clearly expressing your thoughts and feelings, even if they differ from your partner's. For example, if you feel pressured to go along with something you're uncomfortable with, you can advocate for yourself by saying, "I understand that this is important to you, but it doesn't align with my values. I need to make a different choice." Self-advocacy helps you maintain your autonomy and ensures that your voice is heard in the relationship.

Reclaiming your power also involves breaking free from the cycle of guilt and obligation that manipulators often create. Manipulators may use tactics like emotional blackmail to make you feel guilty for asserting your needs or setting boundaries. They may suggest that you are being selfish or unreasonable, causing you to question your own actions. It's important to recognize these tactics for what they are, attempts to control and manipulate your emotions. Reclaiming your power means refusing to be swayed by guilt or obligation and standing firm in your decisions. Remind yourself that you have the right to prioritize your own well-being and that taking care of yourself is not selfish.

In addition to setting boundaries and making independent decisions, building self-confidence is a key part of reclaiming your power. Manipulators often target individuals with low self-esteem because they are more likely to doubt themselves and give in to manipulation. By building your self-confidence, you strengthen your ability to resist manipulation and assert your needs. One way to build self-confidence is by focusing on your strengths and accomplishments. Take time to reflect on the things you've achieved and the qualities that make you unique. Celebrate your successes, no matter how small, and remind yourself that you are capable and deserving of respect.

Another way to build self-confidence is by surrounding yourself with supportive people who uplift and encourage you. Friends, family members, or support groups can provide valuable perspective and reassurance, helping you see the situation more clearly and reinforcing your sense of self-worth. Having a strong support system can also give you the courage to stand up to manipulation and make decisions that are in your best interest.

It's also important to practice self-care as you work to reclaim your power. Self-care involves taking intentional actions to nurture your physical, emotional, and mental well-being. This might include activities like exercise, meditation, spending time in nature, or engaging in hobbies that bring you joy. Self-care helps you stay grounded and resilient in the face of manipulation, making it easier to maintain your boundaries and assert your needs. Additionally, self-care reinforces the idea that you are worthy of love and care, both from yourself and others.

As you reclaim your power, it's essential to keep in mind that this process is not always easy or straightforward. You may encounter resistance from the manipulator, or you may struggle with feelings of doubt or fear. It's important to be patient with yourself and recognize that reclaiming your power is a journey, not a destination. There may be setbacks along the way, but each step you take towards asserting your autonomy is a victory. Remember that you have the right to live a life free from manipulation, and that reclaiming your power is an act of self-respect and self-love.

In some cases, reclaiming your power may involve making the difficult decision to leave the relationship. If the manipulation is severe or if your boundaries continue to be violated despite your best efforts, it may be necessary to remove yourself from the situation in order to protect your well-being. Leaving a manipulative relationship can be challenging, but it is also an opportunity to reclaim your life and rebuild your sense of self. If you decide to leave, seek support from trusted friends, family, or a therapist to help you navigate the process and stay safe.

Reclaiming your power in a relationship with a manipulator involves setting and enforcing boundaries, making independent decisions, building self-confidence, and practicing self-care. By taking these steps, you can regain control of your life and create a healthier, more fulfilling relationship dynamic. Remember that you deserve to be treated with respect and that reclaiming your power is an essential part of protecting your well-being and happiness.

Building Emotional Resilience

Building emotional resilience is a vital skill that helps you navigate and withstand the challenges of manipulation in relationships. Emotional resilience is your ability to adapt to stress, adversity, and challenging situations without being overwhelmed by them. When you build emotional resilience, you strengthen your capacity to stay grounded, think clearly, and maintain your sense of self, even in the face of manipulation. Techniques such as positive self-talk, self-care, and seeking support are key components in developing this resilience.

One of the first steps in building emotional resilience is cultivating positive self-talk. Positive self-talk refers to the inner dialogue that you have with yourself. This dialogue can either uplift you or bring you down, depending on whether it is positive or negative. When you engage in positive self-talk, you challenge and replace negative thoughts with constructive and affirming ones. For example, instead of thinking, "I'm not good enough," you might remind yourself, "I am capable and strong, and I can handle this situation." This shift in perspective can greatly impact how you perceive yourself and your ability to cope with challenges.

Positive self-talk also helps counteract the negative messages that manipulators may try to instill in you. Manipulators often use tactics like criticism, blame, or belittlement to undermine your self-esteem and make you doubt yourself. By practicing positive self-talk, you reinforce your own worth and reject the negative labels that others may try to impose on you. For instance, if a manipulator tries to make you feel guilty for setting a boundary, you can remind yourself, "It's okay to take care of myself and prioritize my needs. Setting boundaries is healthy and necessary." Over time, positive self-talk can help you build a strong inner foundation that supports your emotional resilience.

Another crucial aspect of building emotional resilience is engaging in regular self-care. Self-care involves taking deliberate actions to care for your physical, emotional, and mental well-being. This can include a wide range of activities, such as exercising, eating nutritious foods, getting enough sleep, practicing mindfulness, and spending time doing things you enjoy. Self-care is not just about indulging in pleasures; it's about making choices that support your overall health and well-being.

When you practice self-care, you're better equipped to handle stress and manipulation. Taking care of your body, for example, can boost your energy levels and improve your mood, making it easier to stay calm and centered during difficult interactions. Emotional self-care, such as journaling or talking to a friend, can help you process your feelings and gain clarity about what you're experiencing. Mental self-care, such as setting aside time for relaxation or meditation, can help you clear your mind and reduce anxiety. By incorporating self-care into your daily routine, you build a reservoir of strength and resilience that you can draw on when faced with manipulation.

Seeking support is another vital technique for building emotional resilience. Having a strong support system of friends, family, or a therapist can provide you with the encouragement and perspective you need to navigate manipulation. Supportive relationships offer a safe space where you can express your feelings, gain insights, and receive validation. When you're dealing with a manipulative relationship, it's easy to feel isolated or misunderstood. A trusted support network can remind you that you're not alone and that others care about your well-being.

Talking to someone you trust can also help you see the situation more clearly. Manipulation often involves confusing or contradictory behavior that can make you doubt your perceptions. A supportive friend or therapist can offer an outside perspective that helps you recognize manipulation for what it is. They can also offer advice, share their own experiences, and provide a listening ear when you need to vent. By seeking support, you strengthen your emotional resilience and gain the confidence to stand up to manipulation.

Another technique for building emotional resilience is practicing mindfulness. Mindfulness involves being fully present in the moment and observing your thoughts and feelings without judgment. When you practice mindfulness, you become more aware of your emotional responses and how they are influenced by external factors, such as manipulation. This awareness allows you to take a step back and respond to situations more calmly and thoughtfully, rather than reacting impulsively.

Mindfulness can be particularly helpful in managing stress and anxiety, which are common reactions to manipulation. For example, if you notice that you're feeling tense or anxious during an interaction with a manipulator, you can use mindfulness techniques, such as deep breathing or grounding exercises, to calm your nervous system. This can help you stay composed and focused, even in challenging situations. By cultivating mindfulness, you build your capacity to navigate manipulation with greater clarity and emotional resilience.

In addition to these techniques, setting realistic expectations for yourself is an important aspect of building emotional resilience. It's important to recognize that building resilience is a gradual process, and it's okay to have setbacks along the way. Being kind and compassionate with yourself during this process is essential. Instead of criticizing yourself for not handling a situation perfectly, acknowledge the effort you're making and the progress you've achieved. Celebrate your successes, no matter how small, and use them as motivation to keep moving forward.

Building emotional resilience involves developing a strong sense of purpose and meaning in your life. When you have a clear sense of your values, goals, and what matters most to you, you're better able to withstand the challenges of manipulation. A strong sense of purpose can serve as an anchor that keeps you grounded, even when others try to undermine your confidence or control your decisions. Whether your sense of purpose comes from your relationships, career, hobbies, or personal growth, having something that gives your life meaning can help you stay focused and resilient in the face of manipulation.

Building emotional resilience to withstand manipulation involves a combination of techniques, including positive self-talk, self-care, seeking support, mindfulness, setting realistic expectations, and developing a strong sense of purpose. By incorporating these practices into your life, you can strengthen your ability to cope with challenges, protect your well-being, and maintain your sense of self in the face of manipulation. Remember that building resilience is an ongoing journey, and each step you take towards greater emotional strength is an important part of your personal growth and empowerment.

CHAPTER 6

Confronting the Manipulator

Effective Communication Strategies

Confronting a manipulator is a delicate process that requires effective communication strategies to address the behavior directly and assertively. When faced with manipulation, it's essential to communicate in a way that asserts your boundaries, conveys your feelings clearly, and challenges the manipulator's tactics without escalating the situation. To do this effectively, you must be prepared with specific approaches that help you maintain control of the conversation, stay calm, and ensure that your message is understood.

The first step in confronting a manipulator is to use "I" statements. "I" statements allow you to express your feelings and thoughts without sounding accusatory, which can prevent the other person from becoming defensive. For example, instead of saying, "You always try to control me," you can say, "I feel uncomfortable when decisions are made without considering my input." This approach shifts the focus from blaming the other person to expressing how their behavior affects you, which can open up a more constructive dialogue.

When using "I" statements, it's important to be specific about the behavior you're addressing. Vague statements can lead to misunderstandings or give the manipulator room to twist your words. For instance, instead of saying, "You're being manipulative," specify the behavior by saying, "I feel pressured when you repeatedly insist on something after I've already said no." By pinpointing the exact behavior, you make it clear what the issue is, making it harder for the manipulator to deflect or deny their actions.

Maintaining a calm and composed demeanor is also crucial when confronting a manipulator.

Manipulators often rely on provoking emotional reactions to gain control of the situation. If you become overly emotional, you may lose focus and the conversation could spiral out of control. To avoid this, take deep breaths and keep your voice steady. If you feel yourself getting upset, it's okay to take a pause and collect your thoughts before continuing. By staying calm, you assert control over the interaction and demonstrate that you're not easily swayed by manipulative tactics.

Another effective communication strategy is to use assertive language. Being assertive means standing up for yourself while respecting the other person's rights. It's a balance between passivity and aggression, where you express your needs and boundaries clearly without being rude or hostile. For example, you can say, "I need to be heard in this conversation, and I expect my opinions to be respected," instead of, "You never listen to me." Assertiveness conveys confidence and self-respect, making it clear that you're not willing to be manipulated.

It's also important to set clear and firm boundaries during the conversation. Manipulators often push limits to see how far they can go, so it's essential to communicate what you will and will not tolerate. For example, you can say, "I'm not comfortable discussing this further until we can have a respectful conversation," or, "I'm willing to compromise, but I will not be pressured into something I don't agree with." Setting boundaries helps to establish the rules of engagement and shows the manipulator that you're serious about protecting your well-being.

When setting boundaries, be prepared for the possibility of pushback. Manipulators may try to test your boundaries by challenging or dismissing them. It's important to stay firm and reiterate your stance if necessary. For example, if the manipulator tries to downplay your concerns, you can respond by saying, "I understand that you may see it differently, but this is important to me, and I need you to respect my boundary." Consistency is key in showing that you're committed to maintaining your boundaries.

Using active listening is another crucial component of effective communication when confronting a manipulator. Active listening involves fully concentrating on what the other person is saying, acknowledging their words, and responding thoughtfully. This doesn't mean agreeing with the manipulator, but rather ensuring that you understand their perspective before responding. You can use phrases like, "I hear that you're concerned about…" or "It sounds like you're saying…" to reflect back what you've heard. This approach can help de-escalate the situation and show that you're engaging in the conversation in good faith.

However, while active listening is important, it's equally important to be aware of any attempts by the manipulator to distract or derail the conversation. Manipulators often use tactics like changing the subject, playing the victim, or introducing irrelevant issues to avoid addressing the main problem. If this happens, gently steer the conversation back to the original issue by saying something like, "I'd like to focus on the main concern here, which is..." This helps you stay on track and ensures that the conversation remains productive.

In addition to these strategies, it's important to stay grounded in your values and beliefs when confronting a manipulator. Manipulators may try to make you question your judgment or second-guess your decisions. By staying true to your values, you can remain confident in your stance and resist being swayed by manipulation. For example, if you value honesty and transparency, you can say, "It's important to me that we're honest with each other, so I need to know that you're being truthful." This reinforces your commitment to your principles and signals that you won't tolerate dishonesty.

Another technique is to practice saying "no" assertively. Manipulators often rely on people-pleasing tendencies to get what they want, so being able to say "no" firmly and without guilt is crucial. When saying "no," it's important to be direct and unapologetic. For example, you can simply say, "No, I'm not comfortable with that," or "No, that doesn't work for me." You don't need to provide a lengthy explanation or justification; a clear and concise "no" is enough to assert your boundaries.

It's important to have an exit strategy if the conversation becomes unproductive or hostile. If you feel that the conversation is going nowhere or that the manipulator is becoming aggressive, it's okay to end the discussion. You can say something like, "I don't think we're going to reach an understanding right now, so I'm going to step away from this conversation." This allows you to protect yourself from further manipulation and shows that you're not willing to engage in a toxic exchange.

Confronting a manipulator requires a combination of effective communication strategies, including using "I" statements, staying calm, being assertive, setting boundaries, active listening, staying true to your values, and knowing when to say "no" or exit the conversation. By employing these techniques, you can address manipulative behavior directly and assertively while maintaining your integrity and self-respect. Remember that confronting manipulation is not about winning an argument, but about standing up for yourself and ensuring that your needs and boundaries are respected.

Navigating the Fallout

Confronting a manipulator is often just the beginning of a challenging process that can lead to significant fallout. Manipulators are usually skilled at maintaining control, and when they feel that control slipping away, they may react in various ways to regain their dominance. Understanding and preparing for the potential backlash is crucial for navigating the aftermath of such a confrontation. This process involves maintaining your resolve, managing emotional responses, and protecting yourself from further manipulation.

One of the first things to expect after confronting a manipulator is an escalation in their tactics. Manipulators often become more aggressive when their usual strategies no longer work. This escalation can take many forms, including increased pressure, emotional outbursts, or attempts to undermine your confidence. They may resort to guilt-tripping, making you feel responsible for the conflict, or even accusing you of being the one who is manipulative. It's important to recognize these behaviors for what they are: attempts to reassert control.

When facing this escalation, it's essential to stay calm and grounded. Manipulators thrive on emotional reactions, as these can be used to manipulate you further. Keeping a clear head allows you to see through their tactics and avoid getting drawn into their drama. One effective way to maintain your composure is by reminding yourself of your initial reasons for confronting the manipulator. Keeping your goals and boundaries in mind can help you stay focused on what's important and prevent you from being swayed by their attempts to shift the narrative.

Another common reaction from manipulators is playing the victim. They may portray themselves as the wronged party, seeking sympathy from others or trying to make you feel guilty for confronting them. This tactic can be particularly challenging because it may involve manipulating mutual friends or family members, turning them against you, or making you appear unreasonable. In such situations, it's crucial to stand by your truth and avoid getting caught up in defending yourself to others. Instead, calmly explain your side of the story to those who matter, without getting entangled in the manipulator's attempts to garner pity.

In addition to playing the victim, manipulators may also use deflection as a way to avoid taking responsibility for their actions. They might bring up unrelated issues, accuse you of faults, or try to confuse the situation by introducing new problems. This tactic is designed to shift the focus away from their behavior and onto something else, making it difficult for you to stay on topic. The key to navigating this challenge is to be persistent in steering the conversation back to the original issue. You can do this by calmly repeating your points and refusing to be sidetracked.

Manipulators might also employ what is known as "gaslighting," a tactic that makes you question your perception of reality. After being confronted, they might deny their behavior, claim that you're imagining things, or suggest that you're overreacting. This can be deeply unsettling, as it can lead to self-doubt and confusion. To counteract gaslighting, it's important to trust your own experiences and feelings. Keeping a journal of incidents or discussing the situation with a trusted friend or therapist can help you stay anchored in reality and resist the manipulator's attempts to distort the truth.

Another possible repercussion of confronting a manipulator is that they may try to isolate you. If they sense that you're becoming independent and less susceptible to their control, they might attempt to cut you off from your support system. This could involve badmouthing you to others, creating rifts between you and people you care about, or making it difficult for you to maintain relationships outside of the one with the manipulator. To navigate this, it's essential to strengthen your connections with others and seek out support from people who understand your situation. Building a strong network of allies can provide the emotional reinforcement you need to withstand the manipulator's attempts at isolation.

In some cases, the manipulator may resort to direct retaliation, which can include verbal abuse, threats, or even attempts to sabotage your personal or professional life. These actions are designed to intimidate you into backing down or regaining their control over you. If you find yourself in such a situation, it's crucial to prioritize your safety. This may mean distancing yourself from the manipulator, seeking legal advice, or involving authorities if necessary. Protecting yourself should always be the top priority when dealing with a manipulator who has become aggressive or dangerous.

Even if the manipulator's retaliation is less overt, the psychological impact can still be significant. You may experience feelings of fear, anxiety, or self-doubt as a result of their actions. To navigate these emotional challenges, it's important to practice self-care and seek professional help if needed. Therapy can be a valuable resource for processing your emotions, rebuilding your confidence, and developing strategies to cope with the ongoing effects of manipulation. Engaging in activities that promote mental and physical well-being, such as exercise, mindfulness, and hobbies, can also help you stay resilient in the face of adversity.

In addition to dealing with the immediate fallout, it's important to consider the long-term implications of confronting a manipulator. Over time, you may need to reevaluate the relationship and decide whether it's healthy or sustainable to continue. If the manipulator shows no signs of changing their behavior, it may be necessary to distance yourself or even end the relationship entirely. This can be a difficult decision, especially if you have deep emotional ties to the person. However, your well-being and mental health should always come first.

If you decide to continue the relationship, setting and maintaining clear boundaries will be essential to protect yourself from future manipulation. This means consistently enforcing the limits you've set and being prepared to walk away if they are not respected. It's also important to continue working on your own self-awareness and emotional resilience, so that you can recognize any attempts at manipulation early and respond effectively.

Navigating the fallout of confronting a manipulator is undoubtedly challenging, but it's also an opportunity for growth and empowerment. By standing up to manipulation and maintaining your boundaries, you reclaim your autonomy and take control of your own life. The process may be difficult, but it ultimately leads to greater self-respect and healthier relationships.

Throughout this journey, it's important to remember that you're not alone. Seeking support from friends, family, or a therapist can provide valuable guidance and encouragement as you navigate the complexities of dealing with a manipulator. Whether you choose to repair the relationship or move on, the experience of confronting and overcoming manipulation can be a powerful catalyst for personal growth and a stronger sense of self.

Confronting a manipulator can lead to various challenges, including backlash, further manipulation, and emotional turmoil. However, by staying calm, maintaining your boundaries, seeking support, and prioritizing your well-being, you can navigate these challenges and emerge stronger. The process may be difficult, but it's an essential step toward reclaiming your power and living a life free from manipulation.

Seeking Support

Dealing with a manipulative relationship can be an isolating and overwhelming experience. When you find yourself caught in the web of manipulation, it's essential to recognize the importance of seeking support from others. Reaching out to friends, family, or professionals can provide you with the strength, perspective, and resources needed to navigate this challenging situation. Knowing when and how to seek help is crucial in protecting your well-being and breaking free from the harmful dynamics of a manipulative relationship.

One of the most critical times to seek support is when you start to feel confused, doubtful, or emotionally drained due to the manipulative behavior of your partner. Manipulators often use tactics like gaslighting, emotional blackmail, and guilt-tripping, which can make you question your reality and feel isolated. If you find that your confidence is eroding, and you are constantly second-guessing yourself, it's a clear sign that you need to reach out to someone you trust. Talking to a friend or family member can help you gain perspective and validate your feelings, reminding you that you are not alone in your experiences.

It's important to choose the right people to confide in. Look for individuals who are empathetic, non-judgmental, and have your best interests at heart. These might be close friends, family members, or even coworkers who have shown understanding and support in the past. When you approach them, it's okay to start by simply sharing your feelings and concerns without diving into the details right away. Sometimes, just having someone listen and acknowledge your pain can be incredibly healing.

When explaining your situation, be as honest and clear as possible about what you're experiencing. It can be helpful to provide specific examples of the manipulative behavior you're facing, so your supporters can better understand the severity of the situation. For instance, you might describe instances where your partner made you feel guilty for setting boundaries, twisted the truth to make you doubt yourself, or isolated you from your social circle.

The more your friends and family understand, the better they can support you.

In some cases, you may encounter people who don't fully grasp the seriousness of your situation or who might dismiss your concerns. This can be disheartening, but it's important to remember that not everyone will understand the complexities of manipulation, especially if they haven't experienced it themselves. If someone reacts this way, don't let it deter you from seeking help. Instead, consider reaching out to another trusted person or professional who might be better equipped to offer the support you need.

Professional help is often a critical resource for those dealing with manipulative relationships. Therapists, counselors, and support groups provide a safe and confidential space to explore your feelings, gain insight into the manipulator's tactics, and develop strategies for coping. A therapist can help you identify patterns of manipulation, work through any emotional trauma, and build resilience. Therapy is particularly beneficial if you're struggling with feelings of guilt, shame, or low self-esteem, as these emotions can make it harder to break free from a manipulative relationship.

When looking for a therapist or counselor, consider someone who specializes in relationships, emotional abuse, or trauma. You can start by asking for recommendations from friends or searching online for professionals in your area. Many therapists offer a free initial consultation, which gives you an opportunity to see if their approach aligns with your needs. It's important to find someone you feel comfortable with, as the therapeutic relationship is built on trust and mutual respect.

Support groups can also be an invaluable resource, especially if you feel isolated or misunderstood by those around you. These groups bring together people who are going through similar experiences, providing a sense of community and shared understanding. Whether in person or online, support groups offer a platform to share your story, receive encouragement, and learn from others who have faced similar challenges. The collective wisdom of the group can be a powerful source of strength and inspiration as you navigate your situation.

In addition to seeking emotional support, you may also need practical assistance, particularly if you're considering leaving the relationship. Manipulative partners often make it difficult to leave by using financial control, threats, or intimidation. If you're in this situation, reaching out to a domestic violence shelter, legal advisor, or financial counselor can help you plan a safe and secure exit strategy. These professionals can provide information on your rights, help you access resources, and support you in making decisions that protect your safety and well-being.

When reaching out for support, it's essential to maintain your privacy and safety, especially if your partner is highly controlling or abusive. Be mindful of how and where you communicate with others about your situation. If possible, use a secure phone or computer, and avoid discussing your plans in places where your partner might overhear. In extreme cases, you may need to develop a safety plan, which could include having a trusted friend or family member on standby to help you if the situation escalates.

While seeking support is a crucial step in dealing with a manipulative relationship, it's also important to recognize that the journey towards healing and empowerment is ongoing. As you receive support and begin to reclaim your sense of self, continue to practice self-care and prioritize your mental and emotional health. This might include setting aside time for activities that bring you joy, engaging in mindfulness practices, or continuing therapy to process your experiences.

Remember, the decision to seek support is a sign of strength, not weakness. It shows that you value yourself and are committed to creating a healthier, more fulfilling life. No one deserves to be manipulated or controlled, and by reaching out to others, you're taking an important step towards breaking free from the cycle of manipulation and reclaiming your power.

Knowing when and how to seek support is vital for anyone dealing with a manipulative relationship. By reaching out to trusted friends, family, or professionals, you can gain the emotional and practical assistance needed to navigate this challenging situation. Whether through therapy, support groups, or legal advice, the right help can empower you to recognize manipulation, set boundaries, and ultimately, find a path to a healthier, more independent life. Your well-being is worth fighting for, and you don't have to face this journey alone.

CHAPTER 7

Healing and Moving Forward

Processing Emotional Trauma

Healing from the emotional trauma caused by manipulation is a complex and personal journey. It requires time, patience, and the right strategies to rebuild your sense of self and regain your emotional well-being. Manipulation can leave deep scars, making it challenging to trust others and yourself again. However, with the right tools and support, it is possible to process this trauma and move forward with a renewed sense of strength and clarity.

One of the most effective ways to begin healing from emotional trauma is through therapy. A trained therapist can provide a safe and supportive environment where you can explore your feelings, understand the impact of the manipulation, and develop strategies for recovery. Therapy allows you to unpack the layers of hurt, confusion, and self-doubt that manipulation often causes. It helps you recognize the patterns that led to the trauma and how to break free from them. Cognitive-behavioral therapy is particularly useful for addressing the negative thoughts and beliefs that manipulators often instill in their victims. Cognitive-behavioral therapy helps you reframe these thoughts, replacing them with more positive and empowering ones.

In addition to traditional therapy, there are other therapeutic practices that can aid in healing from emotional trauma. One such practice is journaling. Writing down your thoughts and emotions can be a powerful tool for processing trauma. Journaling allows you to express your feelings in a safe space without fear of judgment. It helps you make sense of your experiences and can reveal patterns or triggers that you might not have noticed otherwise. Regular journaling can also help you track your progress over time, giving you a tangible way to see how far you've come in your healing journey.

When journaling, it's important to write freely and honestly. You might start by simply recording what happened, how it made you feel, and how those feelings have evolved over time. As you continue to journal, you may find it helpful to explore deeper questions, such as what you've learned from the experience or how you can protect yourself from similar situations in the future. Some people find it beneficial to use prompts or guided journals specifically designed for trauma recovery, as these can help direct your thoughts in a constructive way.

Another valuable practice for healing from emotional trauma is mindfulness. Mindfulness involves staying present in the moment and observing your thoughts and feelings without judgment. It can help you become more aware of the ways in which trauma affects you in your daily life, allowing you to address those impacts more effectively. Mindfulness techniques such as deep breathing, meditation, and progressive muscle relaxation can help calm the mind and reduce anxiety, making it easier to process your emotions.

Practicing self-compassion is also crucial in the healing process. Manipulation often leaves victims feeling unworthy, ashamed, or guilty, and these feelings can be barriers to recovery. Self-compassion involves treating yourself with the same kindness and understanding that you would offer a friend who is going through a tough time. It means recognizing that you are not to blame for the manipulation and that your feelings are valid. By being gentle with yourself and acknowledging your pain, you create an environment in which healing can occur.

Connecting with others who have had similar experiences can be incredibly healing as well. Support groups, whether in person or online, provide a space where you can share your story and hear from others who have faced similar challenges. These connections can reduce feelings of isolation and provide a sense of community. In a support group, you can gain insight from others' experiences and learn new coping strategies. Hearing from others who have successfully moved on from similar situations can also give you hope and motivation in your own healing journey.

In addition to emotional and mental healing, it's important to focus on your physical well-being. Trauma can take a toll on the body, leading to symptoms like fatigue, headaches, or digestive issues. Taking care of your physical health by eating well, getting enough sleep, and engaging in regular physical activity can support your overall recovery. Exercise, in particular, has been shown to reduce symptoms of anxiety and depression, both of which are common after experiencing manipulation.

As you work through the emotional trauma, it's important to set realistic expectations for yourself.

Healing is not a linear process, and there will likely be ups and downs along the way. You might have days where you feel strong and confident, followed by days where the pain feels fresh again. This is normal, and it doesn't mean that you're not making progress. It's important to celebrate the small victories and be patient with yourself during setbacks.

Another key aspect of healing is rebuilding your sense of identity and self-worth. Manipulation often strips away a person's sense of self, leaving them feeling lost or unsure of who they are. Reconnecting with your passions, hobbies, and interests can help you rediscover your identity. Engage in activities that make you feel happy and fulfilled, whether that's painting, hiking, reading, or volunteering. These activities can remind you of your strengths and help you rebuild your confidence.

Forgiveness, both of yourself and the manipulator, can also play a role in the healing process.

Forgiveness doesn't mean condoning the manipulator's actions or forgetting what happened. Instead, it's about releasing the hold that the anger and resentment have on you. Holding onto these negative emotions can keep you stuck in the past and prevent you from moving forward. By forgiving yourself for any perceived mistakes and forgiving the manipulator for their actions, you free yourself from the burden of the past and open the door to healing.

As you continue on your healing journey, it's important to keep building and maintaining a support system. Surround yourself with people who respect and care for you, and who support your growth and recovery. This support system can provide you with encouragement, perspective, and love as you move forward. Don't be afraid to lean on them when you need to, and remember that asking for help is a sign of strength, not weakness.

In conclusion, healing from the emotional trauma of manipulation is a journey that requires time, effort, and the right tools. Therapy, journaling, mindfulness, and self-compassion are all valuable practices that can help you process your emotions and move forward. Reconnecting with your identity, seeking support, and practicing forgiveness are also essential steps in the healing process. By taking these steps, you can begin to rebuild your sense of self, regain your confidence, and create a future that is free from the pain of the past.

Rebuilding Trust

Rebuilding trust after experiencing manipulation is a challenging but essential part of the healing process. Manipulation often erodes trust, not only in others but also in oneself. When someone has manipulated you, it can leave you questioning your judgment, doubting your instincts, and feeling wary of future relationships. However, with patience, effort, and the right strategies, it is possible to restore faith in yourself and in others, paving the way for healthier and more fulfilling relationships.

One of the first steps in rebuilding trust is to reconnect with yourself. Manipulation can create deep-seated doubts about your ability to make sound decisions or recognize when something is wrong. To rebuild trust in yourself, it's important to start by acknowledging the pain and confusion caused by the manipulation, rather than suppressing or dismissing it. Give yourself permission to feel and express the emotions that come with that experience; whether it's anger, sadness, or fear. These feelings are valid and part of your healing journey.

To regain trust in your own judgment, begin by reflecting on past situations where you made good decisions. Remind yourself of times when you trusted your instincts and they served you well. This exercise can help rebuild your confidence in your ability to make sound choices. Additionally, practice tuning into your intuition. When you're faced with decisions, big or small, pause and listen to what your gut is telling you. Over time, this practice will help you trust your instincts more and reinforce the belief that you can rely on yourself.

Another important aspect of rebuilding trust in yourself is setting and honoring personal boundaries. Boundaries are essential in protecting your well-being and ensuring that you feel safe and respected in your relationships. After experiencing manipulation, it's common to question your ability to set effective boundaries. Start by clearly identifying what your boundaries are. These might include limits on how you allow others to treat you, what behaviors are acceptable, and what you need to feel secure in a relationship. Once you've identified your boundaries, communicate them clearly and assertively to others. Remember, it's okay to say no and to stand up for your needs. Each time you enforce a boundary, you strengthen your trust in yourself.

Restoring trust in others, especially after being manipulated, can be a slower process. It's natural to feel guarded or skeptical about new relationships, but it's important not to let the past dictate your future. Begin by recognizing that not everyone is like the person who manipulated you. There are people who are kind, respectful, and trustworthy. Rebuilding trust in others involves giving yourself the time and space to observe and get to know someone without rushing into a relationship. Pay attention to their actions, not just their words, as consistent behavior over time is a key indicator of trustworthiness.

It's also helpful to start with small steps when rebuilding trust in others. Begin by trusting others with low-risk situations. This might involve sharing something small about yourself or relying on someone for a minor favor. As you see that your trust is being honored, gradually increase the level of trust you place in that person. This gradual approach helps to rebuild your confidence in others without overwhelming you.

Effective communication is crucial in rebuilding trust in relationships. Open, honest, and clear communication helps prevent misunderstandings and builds a strong foundation of trust. When entering new relationships or repairing old ones, make a conscious effort to communicate your thoughts, feelings, and expectations clearly. Encourage the other person to do the same. This transparency helps both parties feel more secure and respected, which is essential for trust to flourish.

Learning to forgive is another important step in rebuilding trust. This doesn't mean condoning the manipulative behavior or forgetting what happened, but rather releasing the hold that anger and resentment have over you. Forgiveness is a way of letting go of the past and freeing yourself from the emotional burden it carries. It allows you to move forward with a lighter heart and an open mind, which are necessary for rebuilding trust. Forgiving yourself is equally important, especially if you feel you were at fault for not recognizing the manipulation sooner. Remember that manipulation is a deliberate act by another person, and it's not your fault. Be kind to yourself and recognize that you did the best you could with the information and resources you had at the time.

Seeking support from others can also play a significant role in rebuilding trust. Talking to friends, family, or a therapist about your experiences and fears can provide you with reassurance and perspective. These supportive relationships can serve as a reminder that trust is possible and that there are people who genuinely care about your well-being. If you're hesitant to open up to others because of past manipulation, start by sharing with those you know have always been reliable and understanding. Their responses can help rebuild your belief in the goodness and trustworthiness of people.

As you work on rebuilding trust, it's important to practice patience with yourself and the process. Healing from the effects of manipulation takes time, and it's normal to experience setbacks or moments of doubt along the way. Be gentle with yourself during these times and remind yourself that rebuilding trust is a gradual process. Celebrate small victories and progress, and don't be discouraged if it takes longer than you expected.

It's also helpful to establish a sense of control in your life as you work on rebuilding trust. This might involve setting personal goals, pursuing hobbies, or taking on new challenges. By focusing on things you can control, you reinforce your sense of agency and self-reliance, which are key components of trust. Each accomplishment, no matter how small, can boost your confidence and remind you of your strengths.

As you rebuild trust, it's important to stay vigilant but not paranoid. While it's essential to be aware of red flags and to protect yourself from potential manipulation, it's also important not to let fear of being hurt again prevent you from forming meaningful relationships. Strive for a balance where you remain cautious and aware, but also open to the possibility of positive and trusting relationships.

Rebuilding trust after experiencing manipulation is a multi-faceted process that requires time, effort, and a commitment to self-growth. It involves reconnecting with yourself, setting and enforcing boundaries, gradually rebuilding trust in others, practicing effective communication, and seeking support. By taking these steps, you can restore your faith in yourself and in others, paving the way for healthier, more fulfilling relationships in the future.

Establishing Healthy Relationships

A healthy relationship is a partnership built on mutual respect, trust, open communication, and shared values. Unlike relationships characterized by manipulation, a healthy relationship allows both individuals to thrive, feel secure, and grow together. Establishing a healthy relationship requires an understanding of what makes a relationship healthy and the qualities to seek in a partner.

One of the key elements of a healthy relationship is mutual respect. In such a relationship, both individuals value each other's opinions, feelings, and boundaries. They recognize that they are equal partners, each deserving of dignity and consideration. This respect is reflected in how they communicate, resolve conflicts, and support one another. When both partners respect each other, there is no room for belittling, demeaning, or controlling behavior. Instead, they uplift and encourage one another, fostering a positive and supportive environment.

Trust is another cornerstone of a healthy relationship. Trust allows partners to feel safe with each other, knowing that they can rely on one another emotionally, physically, and mentally. In a trusting relationship, both partners are honest and transparent, keeping no secrets that could harm the relationship. They trust each other's intentions and actions, which reduces feelings of jealousy, insecurity, or doubt. Trust is not built overnight; it develops over time through consistent actions, honesty, and reliability. In a healthy relationship, trust is maintained by being faithful to promises, being open about concerns, and addressing issues directly without deception.

Open communication is essential for a healthy relationship. This means both partners are comfortable expressing their thoughts, feelings, and needs without fear of judgment or retaliation. Effective communication involves both speaking and listening. When issues arise, partners in a healthy relationship address them constructively, seeking to understand each other's perspectives and find solutions together. They avoid blaming or accusing each other, instead focusing on resolving conflicts in a way that benefits the relationship as a whole. Open communication also means sharing joys, successes, and dreams, creating a deeper emotional connection and understanding between partners.

Emotional support is another vital component of a healthy relationship. In such a relationship, partners are there for each other during both good and challenging times. They offer encouragement, comfort, and understanding, helping each other navigate life's ups and downs. This emotional support strengthens the bond between partners and reinforces their commitment to one another. It also ensures that both individuals feel valued and cared for, contributing to their overall well-being.

In addition to emotional support, a healthy relationship is characterized by a sense of individuality and independence. While partners share their lives and experiences, they also maintain their own identities, interests, and friendships. They understand that being in a relationship doesn't mean losing oneself but rather sharing life with someone else while continuing to grow as an individual. In a healthy relationship, both partners encourage each other's personal growth and respect each other's need for space and time alone.

Another important aspect of a healthy relationship is equality. Both partners should have an equal say in decisions that affect the relationship. This includes decisions about finances, living arrangements, future plans, and even day-to-day activities. Equality ensures that neither partner feels dominated or controlled by the other, and that both feel their opinions and desires are valued. In a healthy relationship, power is shared, and both partners work together as a team.

Boundaries are crucial in establishing and maintaining a healthy relationship. Boundaries define what is acceptable and unacceptable behavior in the relationship, and they protect both partners' well-being. Healthy boundaries might include respecting each other's privacy, agreeing on how to handle disagreements, and maintaining a balance between time spent together and apart. When both partners set and respect boundaries, they create a safe space where both can feel comfortable and secure.

To establish a healthy relationship, it's important to look for certain qualities in a partner. One of the most important qualities is emotional maturity. A partner who is emotionally mature understands their own emotions and is capable of handling them in a healthy way. They are able to manage stress, communicate effectively, and take responsibility for their actions. Emotional maturity also means being able to empathize with others, which is crucial for building a strong, supportive relationship.

Another important quality to look for in a partner is integrity. A partner with integrity is honest, reliable, and consistent in their actions and words. They do what they say they will do and are trustworthy in both small and significant matters. Integrity ensures that the relationship is built on a foundation of trust and honesty, which is essential for its long-term success.

A good partner should also be supportive. This means they encourage your personal growth, celebrate your successes, and stand by you during difficult times. A supportive partner is someone who genuinely cares about your well-being and is willing to put effort into helping you achieve your goals. They are your cheerleader and your confidant, always ready to offer a listening ear or a helping hand.

Empathy is another key quality to look for in a partner. A partner who is empathetic can understand and share your feelings, even if they haven't experienced the same situation. Empathy allows them to be compassionate and considerate, making them more likely to treat you with kindness and respect. In a healthy relationship, empathy helps both partners connect on a deeper emotional level and strengthens their bond.

Good communication skills are also essential in a partner. Look for someone who can express themselves clearly and who listens attentively when you speak. A partner with good communication skills will be able to discuss issues openly, resolve conflicts in a healthy manner, and ensure that both of you are on the same page regarding important matters. Communication is the glue that holds a relationship together, so having a partner who excels in this area is crucial.

Respect is another vital quality to seek in a partner. A respectful partner values you as an individual and treats you with dignity and consideration. They respect your opinions, beliefs, and boundaries, and they don't engage in behavior that is demeaning or dismissive. Respect is the foundation of any healthy relationship, and without it, the relationship is likely to become unbalanced and unhealthy.

A healthy relationship requires a partner who shares similar values and goals. While it's okay to have differences, it's important that both partners agree on fundamental issues such as family, career aspirations, finances, and lifestyle choices. Shared values and goals create a sense of alignment and purpose in the relationship, making it easier to navigate challenges and work toward a common future.

Establishing a healthy relationship requires both partners to cultivate and maintain mutual respect, trust, open communication, emotional support, individuality, equality, and clear boundaries. When looking for a partner, seek out qualities such as emotional maturity, integrity, supportiveness, empathy, good communication skills, respect, and shared values. By prioritizing these elements, you can build a relationship that is free from manipulation and that fosters growth, happiness, and fulfillment for both partners.

CHAPTER 8

Prevention Strategies

Strengthening Personal Boundaries

Creating and enforcing strong personal boundaries is essential for maintaining healthy relationships and preventing manipulation. Boundaries are the limits we set to protect our well-being, ensure mutual respect, and define what is acceptable and unacceptable in our interactions with others. Establishing clear boundaries helps us maintain our autonomy, self-respect, and emotional health.

The first step in strengthening personal boundaries is understanding your own needs, values, and limits. This self-awareness allows you to identify what behaviors, actions, or words you are comfortable with and what you are not. It's important to take the time to reflect on past experiences where you felt uncomfortable, disrespected, or manipulated. These reflections can help you recognize patterns and understand what kinds of boundaries need to be set in the future.

Once you've identified your boundaries, it's crucial to communicate them clearly and assertively. Clear communication means expressing your boundaries in a straightforward manner, without ambiguity. For example, if a friend frequently borrows your belongings without asking, you could say, "I value my personal space and belongings. Please ask for my permission before taking anything." This statement clearly communicates your boundary and sets the expectation for future behavior.

Assertiveness is key to enforcing boundaries. Being assertive means standing up for yourself in a respectful yet firm way. It involves expressing your needs and limits confidently, without feeling guilty or apologetic. For instance, if someone continuously interrupts you during conversations, you might say, "I appreciate your enthusiasm, but I need to finish my thoughts before we move on. Please allow me to speak without interruption." This response is both respectful and firm, making it clear that your boundary should be respected.

Another important aspect of boundary-setting is consistency. To effectively enforce boundaries, you must be consistent in upholding them. If you allow others to cross your boundaries without consequence, it sends a message that your boundaries are flexible or negotiable. For example, if you've set a boundary that you won't respond to work emails after 8 p.m., but then you do so occasionally, it undermines the boundary. Consistency in maintaining your boundaries helps others understand that you are serious about them and that they should be respected.

It's also essential to recognize that setting boundaries may lead to some pushback or resistance, especially if others are used to overstepping your limits. When this happens, it's important to remain firm and not give in to pressure. For instance, if a family member tries to guilt you into doing something that crosses your boundary, you can respond by reiterating your boundary calmly and firmly, saying, "I understand that you're upset, but I've made my decision based on what's best for me. I hope you can respect that." Standing your ground reinforces your boundary and signals that it is non-negotiable.

Boundaries are not only about saying "no" to others; they are also about saying "yes" to yourself. By setting boundaries, you prioritize your own well-being, self-respect, and mental health. This self-care is crucial in preventing manipulation because it ensures that you are not sacrificing your own needs or values to please others. For example, if you need time alone to recharge after a busy day, it's important to communicate this to others and take the necessary time for yourself, even if others want your attention.

In addition to setting boundaries with others, it's also important to set internal boundaries with yourself. Internal boundaries involve managing your own thoughts, emotions, and behaviors to stay aligned with your values and goals. For instance, if you have a tendency to overcommit yourself, setting an internal boundary might involve reminding yourself to only take on what you can realistically handle. This helps prevent burnout and ensures that you are not compromising your own well-being.

When setting boundaries, it's helpful to use "I" statements, which focus on your own feelings and needs rather than blaming or accusing others. For example, instead of saying, "You're always ignoring me," you could say, "I feel hurt when my opinions are overlooked. I need to feel heard in our conversations." This approach reduces defensiveness in others and emphasizes your personal experience, making it easier for them to understand and respect your boundary.

Boundaries also need to be adaptable and revisited over time. As relationships evolve, so do our needs and limits. It's important to regularly assess whether your boundaries are still serving you and adjust them if necessary. For example, as a relationship deepens, you might feel comfortable allowing more access to your personal space or time. Conversely, if someone consistently disrespects your boundaries, you might need to strengthen them or create new ones to protect yourself.

In some cases, setting boundaries may involve creating physical or emotional distance from individuals who are consistently manipulative or disrespectful. This distance can provide the space needed to protect your well-being and regain a sense of control. For example, if a coworker frequently belittles your work, you might choose to limit your interactions with them or seek support from a supervisor. Distance can help reduce the impact of toxic behavior and give you the clarity needed to uphold your boundaries.

It's also important to recognize that boundary-setting is a skill that takes time and practice to develop. It's normal to feel uncomfortable or unsure when first establishing boundaries, especially if you've been used to accommodating others at your own expense. However, with practice, setting and enforcing boundaries becomes easier and more natural. It's a vital skill for maintaining healthy, respectful relationships and preventing manipulation.

Remember that boundaries are about protecting yourself, not punishing others. The goal is to create a relationship dynamic where both parties feel respected and valued. When boundaries are communicated and enforced in a healthy way, they contribute to a more positive and balanced relationship, where everyone's needs are acknowledged and addressed.

Strengthening personal boundaries is essential for preventing manipulation and maintaining healthy relationships. It involves understanding your own needs and limits, communicating them clearly and assertively, and being consistent in upholding them. By prioritizing your well-being, using "I" statements, and adapting boundaries as needed, you create a relationship environment where respect and mutual understanding thrive. Developing this skill takes practice, but it is a crucial step in ensuring that your relationships are based on respect, equality, and genuine connection.

Cultivating Self-Respect and Confidence

Self-respect and confidence play crucial roles in preventing manipulation and maintaining healthy, fulfilling relationships. These traits act as internal safeguards, helping individuals recognize their worth, stand firm in their beliefs, and resist attempts to control or undermine them. Cultivating self-respect and confidence is not just about feeling good about oneself; it is about developing a deep sense of personal value that can protect against manipulation and ensure healthy interactions with others.

Self-respect is the foundation upon which all healthy relationships are built. It involves recognizing your intrinsic value as a person, regardless of external validation or the opinions of others. When you have self-respect, you understand that your thoughts, feelings, and needs are important and deserve to be treated with dignity. This understanding naturally leads to setting boundaries and standing up for yourself when others attempt to cross them. For example, if someone tries to belittle or demean you, self-respect gives you the strength to assertively reject that behavior and protect your emotional well-being.

Cultivating self-respect begins with self-awareness. It requires taking the time to reflect on your values, strengths, and beliefs. By understanding what is important to you and what you stand for, you create a solid sense of identity that is less susceptible to being swayed by others. This self-awareness also helps you identify situations where you may be compromising your values or self-worth, allowing you to make adjustments that align more closely with your true self.

One effective way to cultivate self-respect is through self-compassion. This involves treating yourself with the same kindness, understanding, and forgiveness that you would offer to a close friend. Instead of harshly criticizing yourself for mistakes or perceived shortcomings, self-compassion encourages you to acknowledge your humanity and embrace your imperfections. For example, if you make a mistake at work, instead of berating yourself, you might say, "I made a mistake, but that doesn't define my worth. I can learn from this and do better next time." This kind approach builds self-respect by reinforcing the idea that you are worthy of love and care, even when you're not perfect.

Confidence, on the other hand, is the belief in your abilities and the assurance that you can handle whatever challenges come your way. It is closely linked to self-respect but focuses more on your capability and competence. When you are confident, you are less likely to be swayed by others' opinions or pressured into doing things that go against your values. Confidence empowers you to take risks, make decisions, and pursue your goals without being deterred by fear or doubt.

Building confidence requires stepping outside your comfort zone and facing challenges head-on. Each time you successfully navigate a difficult situation, your confidence grows. For instance, if you're nervous about speaking up in a meeting, doing so, even if it's just to share a small idea can boost your confidence. Over time, these small acts of courage accumulate, helping you feel more self-assured and less susceptible to manipulation.

Another key aspect of cultivating confidence is positive self-talk. The way you speak to yourself internally has a profound impact on how you perceive yourself and your abilities. Negative self-talk, such as thoughts like "I'm not good enough" or "I always mess things up," undermines confidence and makes you more vulnerable to manipulation. On the other hand, positive self-talk reinforces your strengths and abilities, creating a more resilient mindset. For example, instead of thinking, "I can't do this," you might say, "This is challenging, but I've faced challenges before and succeeded. I can handle this."

Confidence also grows through practice and preparation. The more you practice a skill or prepare for a situation, the more confident you become. For example, if you have an important presentation, practicing it multiple times beforehand will help you feel more confident when the time comes. This preparation reduces anxiety and increases your belief in your ability to succeed, making you less likely to be manipulated by others' doubts or criticisms.

Surrounding yourself with supportive people is another crucial element in building self-respect and confidence. Positive relationships with friends, family, or mentors who believe in you and encourage your growth can have a significant impact on your self-perception. These individuals provide reinforcement when you doubt yourself and offer constructive feedback that helps you grow. They also serve as role models, demonstrating how self-respect and confidence can be lived out in daily life.

It's important to recognize that building self-respect and confidence is a gradual process. It doesn't happen overnight, and there will be setbacks along the way. However, each small step you take towards valuing yourself and believing in your abilities contributes to a stronger foundation that can withstand manipulation. For example, each time you stand up for yourself, even in small ways, you strengthen your self-respect. Each time you tackle a challenge, no matter how minor, you build your confidence.

Self-respect and confidence also involve being assertive about your needs and desires. Assertiveness is the ability to express your thoughts and feelings honestly and directly, while also respecting the rights of others. It's about finding a balance between standing up for yourself and being considerate of others' perspectives. For instance, if you need time to yourself but a friend keeps pressuring you to hang out, being assertive might involve saying, "I appreciate your invitation, but I really need some time to recharge. Let's plan for another day." This approach allows you to honor your own needs without dismissing your friend's feelings.

It's important to celebrate your achievements, no matter how small. Recognizing and celebrating your successes reinforces the belief that you are capable and worthy. This could be as simple as acknowledging a job well done after completing a task or treating yourself to something special after reaching a goal. Celebrating your achievements helps solidify your self-respect and confidence, making you less likely to tolerate manipulation.

Self-respect and confidence are essential tools in preventing manipulation and maintaining healthy relationships. By cultivating these traits, individuals can protect themselves from being controlled or undermined by others. This involves developing self-awareness, practicing self-compassion, engaging in positive self-talk, and surrounding oneself with supportive relationships. As self-respect and confidence grow, so does the ability to set boundaries, make decisions, and pursue goals without being swayed by external pressures. This empowerment is crucial in creating a life that is true to your values and free from manipulation.

Maintaining Vigilance

Maintaining vigilance in future relationships is essential for avoiding manipulative dynamics and ensuring that your connections are healthy, supportive, and respectful. While it's important to approach relationships with an open heart, it's equally crucial to keep your eyes wide open to the signs that something might be off. By staying aware and informed, you can protect yourself from falling into patterns of manipulation again.

One of the first signs to watch for is a lack of respect for your boundaries. In any healthy relationship, your personal limits should be acknowledged and respected without question. If someone frequently dismisses, challenges, or ignores your boundaries, it's a red flag. This might start subtly, with small requests or actions that make you uncomfortable, but it can escalate over time.

For example, if you've expressed a need for space or time alone and the other person constantly intrudes, this disregard for your boundaries signals a potential for manipulation. To remain vigilant, remind yourself that your boundaries are valid, and any repeated violation of them is not something to overlook.

Another key sign of potential manipulation is excessive control or possessiveness. A healthy relationship thrives on mutual respect and trust, where both parties feel free to be themselves without fear of being controlled. If you notice your partner or friend trying to dictate who you spend time with, what you wear, or how you spend your money, this controlling behavior is a warning sign. Manipulators often try to isolate their victims from others to gain more control, so it's crucial to recognize when someone is attempting to cut you off from your support network. Trust your instincts if you feel like you're losing your independence or if you're being coerced into actions or decisions that don't feel right.

Pay attention to the balance of power in your relationships. Healthy relationships are built on equality, where both people have an equal say in decisions and feel valued. If you find that one person is consistently dominating conversations, making all the decisions, or invalidating your opinions, this imbalance of power could indicate manipulation. Manipulators often use tactics like gaslighting, where they make you doubt your own perceptions or reality, to maintain control. For example, if you express concern about something that happened, and the other person dismisses it as you "overreacting" or "imagining things," this could be a form of gaslighting. Staying vigilant means recognizing these power imbalances and trusting your own judgment.

Emotional manipulation can also come in the form of guilt-tripping or playing the victim. If someone frequently makes you feel guilty for not doing things their way or for asserting your needs, this is a manipulation tactic. They may use phrases like, "After all I've done for you" or "If you really loved me, you would..." to coerce you into complying with their wishes. This tactic preys on your empathy and desire to please others, making it difficult to see the manipulation for what it is. To guard against this, it's important to recognize when guilt is being used as a tool to control you and to remind yourself that your feelings and needs are just as important.

Another sign to be aware of is inconsistent behavior or mixed signals. Manipulators often keep you off balance by switching between kindness and cruelty, affection and neglect. This inconsistency can make you feel confused and anxious, constantly questioning where you stand in the relationship. For example, if your partner is loving and attentive one day but cold and distant the next, this unpredictability might be a tactic to keep you dependent on their approval. To maintain vigilance, notice these patterns and consider how they make you feel. A healthy relationship should provide stability, not constant uncertainty.

Financial control is another tactic that manipulators use to exert power. This can include controlling access to money, dictating how you spend your finances, or making you financially dependent on them. If someone insists on managing your finances without your input or creates situations where you feel trapped due to financial dependence, this is a serious red flag. Protecting yourself involves maintaining financial independence and being cautious of any attempts to control your economic resources.

Monitoring how you feel in the relationship is also an important aspect of staying vigilant. Manipulative relationships often leave you feeling drained, anxious, or unsure of yourself. If you frequently feel like you're walking on eggshells, constantly second-guessing your actions or words, it could be a sign that you're being manipulated. Trust your emotional responses; they are valuable indicators of whether a relationship is healthy or harmful. If a relationship consistently makes you feel worse about yourself or leaves you feeling emotionally exhausted, it's time to reassess and possibly remove yourself from that situation.

It's also crucial to be aware of how conflicts are handled in the relationship. Healthy relationships involve open, honest communication where both parties feel heard and respected, even when there's disagreement. Manipulators, however, often avoid direct communication, instead using passive-aggressive behavior, silent treatment, or emotional outbursts to control the situation. For example, if a disagreement leads to the other person shutting down or refusing to discuss the issue, this lack of communication can be a form of manipulation. To protect yourself, insist on respectful, open communication and recognize when conflict is being used as a tool for control.

Keeping a supportive network of friends and family is vital for maintaining vigilance in relationships. Manipulators often try to isolate their victims, making it harder for them to seek outside perspectives. Regularly engaging with your support network allows you to gain insights and feedback that can help you recognize manipulation. If your loved ones express concern about your relationship, take their observations seriously. They might notice things that you have become too close to see. Maintaining these connections also provides a safety net if you need to leave a manipulative relationship.

Staying informed and educated about manipulation tactics is one of the best ways to remain vigilant. The more you know about how manipulators operate, the better equipped you are to recognize the signs early on. Reading books, attending workshops, or seeking therapy can all help you develop a deeper understanding of manipulation and how to protect yourself from it. Knowledge is power, and staying informed gives you the tools to maintain healthy, respectful relationships.

Staying vigilant in future relationships requires a combination of self-awareness, knowledge, and a strong support network. By recognizing the signs of manipulation; such as disrespect for boundaries, control, power imbalances, guilt-tripping, and inconsistent behavior you can protect yourself from falling into harmful dynamics. Trust your instincts, maintain your independence, and don't hesitate to seek support if you feel something isn't right. Healthy relationships are built on mutual respect, trust, and open communication, and by staying vigilant, you can ensure that your relationships are positive and fulfilling.

CONCLUSION

Empowerment and independence are crucial for living a life free from manipulation and filled with healthier, more fulfilling relationships. These qualities don't just emerge overnight; they are cultivated through continuous personal growth, resilience, and a commitment to self-awareness. As you move forward, maintaining your empowerment and independence requires a proactive approach to your well-being and relationships.

One of the most important aspects of maintaining empowerment is committing to ongoing personal growth. Personal growth is not a destination but a continuous journey of self-discovery, learning, and improvement. It involves regularly assessing your values, goals, and boundaries, ensuring they align with the person you want to be. This might mean setting aside time for reflection, journaling about your experiences, or engaging in activities that challenge and expand your understanding of yourself and the world around you.

Resilience plays a critical role in this process. Life will always present challenges, including difficult relationships or situations where manipulation could re-enter your life. Resilience is the ability to bounce back from these challenges, to learn from them, and to emerge stronger. Building resilience involves cultivating a positive mindset, where you see obstacles as opportunities for growth rather than insurmountable problems. This shift in perspective can empower you to face any difficulties head-on, with the confidence that you can overcome them.

A key component of resilience is emotional regulation. Being able to manage your emotions effectively ensures that you remain grounded and clear-headed in the face of manipulation. Techniques such as mindfulness, deep breathing, and positive self-talk can help you stay calm and focused, even in stressful situations. By mastering these skills, you become less susceptible to emotional manipulation, as you can maintain control over your reactions and decisions.

To maintain your empowerment and independence, it's essential to continue setting and reinforcing your personal boundaries. Boundaries are the limits you set to protect your well-being and ensure that your needs are respected in any relationship. Clear, assertive boundary-setting allows you to define what is acceptable and what is not, giving you control over your interactions with others. This is particularly important in preventing manipulation, as those who attempt to manipulate often push against boundaries to see how far they can go. By consistently enforcing your boundaries, you send a clear message that you will not tolerate disrespect or control.

Another important step is to surround yourself with supportive, positive relationships. The people you choose to keep in your life should respect your independence and encourage your growth. Healthy relationships are built on mutual respect, trust, and a shared commitment to each other's well-being. These relationships act as a buffer against manipulation, as they provide a safe space where you can be yourself without fear of being controlled or undermined. Regularly assess your relationships, and be willing to distance yourself from those who do not support your empowerment.

Visualization is a powerful tool for maintaining your empowerment and independence. By visualizing the kind of life you want to lead and the relationships you want to have, you can create a mental roadmap that guides your decisions and actions. Picture yourself in relationships where you feel respected, valued, and free to be yourself. Imagine the joy and fulfillment that come from being in such positive environments. This visualization can serve as motivation to seek out and cultivate these types of relationships, while also helping you recognize when a relationship does not meet these standards.

Striving toward a future filled with healthier, more fulfilling relationships requires a commitment to self-love and self-care. Taking care of your physical, emotional, and mental health should always be a priority. Self-care practices such as regular exercise, healthy eating, meditation, and hobbies that bring you joy can significantly boost your well-being and confidence. When you prioritize your self-care, you are better equipped to handle life's challenges and less likely to fall prey to manipulation.

Another important aspect of maintaining your empowerment is to stay informed and educated. Knowledge is a powerful tool in protecting yourself from manipulation. Continue to educate yourself about healthy relationships, communication skills, and manipulation tactics. The more you know, the better prepared you are to identify and avoid unhealthy dynamics. Consider reading books, attending workshops, or seeking professional guidance to deepen your understanding of these topics.

Developing a strong sense of self-worth is fundamental to maintaining independence. When you value yourself, you are less likely to tolerate behavior that diminishes your sense of worth. Cultivate self-worth by celebrating your achievements, acknowledging your strengths, and being kind to yourself. Avoid negative self-talk and practice affirmations that reinforce your value and capabilities. The stronger your self-worth, the more empowered you will feel to stand up for yourself in any situation.

Moving forward, it's also important to remain open to new experiences and relationships, but with a discerning eye. While it's natural to want to trust others, it's equally important to protect yourself by being cautious. Take the time to get to know people and pay attention to how they make you feel. Trust is something that should be earned over time, not given blindly. By being mindful of this, you can build relationships that are based on mutual respect and trust, rather than falling into manipulative dynamics.

Maintaining your empowerment and independence also involves making decisions that align with your values and goals. Don't be afraid to make choices that are best for you, even if they go against what others might want or expect. Independence means taking ownership of your life and being confident in the decisions you make. Whether it's choosing a career path, deciding who to spend time with, or setting boundaries in relationships, trust yourself to make the right choices for your well-being.

Always seek support when needed. Independence doesn't mean doing everything on your own; it means knowing when to ask for help. Surround yourself with a network of people who support your growth and are there for you when times get tough. Whether it's friends, family, or a professional, having someone to talk to can provide invaluable support and perspective.

Maintaining empowerment and independence is a continuous process of self-awareness, personal growth, and resilience. By setting strong boundaries, surrounding yourself with supportive relationships, and staying informed, you can protect yourself from manipulation and create a life filled with healthy, fulfilling relationships. Visualize the future you want, prioritize your self-care, and always stay true to your values and goals. With these steps, you can confidently move forward, empowered to live a life that is truly your own.